READ'S
MUSICAL RECITER

lids lifted, stones turned, tales told,
stars stripped, rock mined, pop plundered
and pseuds cornered

by

MIKE READ
AND RICHARD HAVERS

SUTTON PUBLISHING

First published in the United Kingdom in 2004 by
Sutton Publishing Limited · Phoenix Mill
Thrupp · Stroud · Gloucestershire · GL5 2BU

British Library Cataloguing in Publication Data
A catalogue record for this book is available from the British Library.

ISBN 0-7509-3889-7

Typeset in 8.5/12 pt Swis721.
Typesetting and origination by
Sutton Publishing Limited.
Printed and bound in England by
J.H. Haynes & Co. Ltd, Sparkford.

reciter ri'saite(r) *n.* a slim yet comprehensive tome pertaining to a particular subject. A cornucopia of the vital and the inconsequential containing stories and anecdotes, facts and lists in an unputdownable melange of the trivial and the profound. Suitable for whiling away the odd spare hour or plundering as the source material for an after-dinner speaking engagement, to enhance your reputation as a raconteur or simply to impress them down the pub.

dwarfed
by the
henge

Back in 1983 former member of Deep Purple Ian Gillan was taking a break from singing about smoke on the water to lend his vocal talents to Black Sabbath.

Ian and Black Sabbath had recorded a new album which they were inspired to call *Born Again*. The album cover featured a baby painted red with two little yellow fangs and rather fetching yellow-painted finger nails – is it any wonder heavy metal prompts the odd raised eyebrow? The band planned to tour North America on the strength of their new album and called a meeting to discuss the stage set, always central to any rock band's live show. In another piece of inspired thinking bass player Geezer Butler suggested that a life-size model of Stonehenge be built and then erected on stage from where the Sabs could entertain their vast legion of fans with some of their new material. Among the tracks on *Born Again* is a 1-minute-58-second, far-from-classic song entitled *Stonehenge*. It sits alongside *Digital Bitch*, *Zero the Hero* and the obligatory title track. All this added up to what is widely regarded as the band's creative nadir.

Thoughts of nadirs, creative or otherwise, were the farthest things from the band's collective consciousness. Week-long rehearsals were arranged at the Maple Leaf hockey stadium in Montreal where the henge set was erected and the band went through their paces. As the week was drawing to a close a dwarf turned up and was promptly dressed in a red leotard and given little yellow fangs to cap his teeth. At the final day's dress rehearsal the said dwarf was placed astride the highest stone and as the music reached a crescendo a pre-recorded scream rang out and the dwarf fell backwards off the henge on to a pile of mattresses that were discreetly placed out of sight of where the audience were to sit. At this point bells started tolling, roadies dressed as monks started crawling across the front of the stage and the wistful tones of Sabbath's 1970 classic track *War Pigs* began. . . . 'HELLO, MONTREAL!'

washboard miracle

For Culture Club's 1984 top 10 hit *It's A Miracle*, Boy George insisted on using a washboard and suggested someone who he thought would be the ideal player. That's how veteran actor Derek Guyler, who'd played the janitor in *The Fenn Street Gang* and Corky in *Sykes*, came to be a featured musician on the hit.

living in the past

On being asked why he had taken to dressing as Sherlock Holmes, Jethro Tull singer Ian Anderson replied, 'I am now twenty-nine and clearly a more sophisticated, older person. By acting like Peter Pan, trying to pretend that I am younger than I am, I would lose credibility with my audience.' That's the best reason ever for taking to a deerstalker and cape.

big time operator

Far from being a lady of leisure, or playing the spouse of a rock star, Buddy Holly's wife Maria Elena Holley (he dropped the 'e' because it looked better) was, at the time of his death in February 1959, still working as switchboard operator in the New York office of the Commonwealth of Puerto Rico.

— SOUNDBITE —

'I think he's an overrated midget.'

KEITH RICHARD ON PRINCE

(before he was the artist formerly known as, and now is again)

what was no.1
on the day . . . ?

Hillary and Tensing became the first men to climb Mount Everest, 1 June 1953 – **FRANKIE LAINE** • *I Believe*

Prince Rainier of Monaco married Grace Kelly, 19 April 1956 – **WINIFRED ATWELL** • *The Poor People of Paris*

The US dropped the first hydrogen bomb at Bikini Atoll, 21 May 1956 – **RONNIE HILTON** • *No Other Love*

The Hungarian revolution broke out, 26 October 1956 – **FRANKIE LAINE** • *A Woman In Love*

Britain's first section of motorway was opened, 5 December 1958 – **LORD ROCKINGHAM'S XI** • *Hoots Mon*

The Dalai Lama found sanctuary in India, 19 April 1959 – **RUSS CONWAY** • *Side Saddle*

Jamaica became independent, 6 August 1962 – **FRANK IFIELD** • *I Remember You*

The Great Train Robbery took place, 8 August 1963 – **THE SEARCHERS** • *Sweets For My Sweet*

John F. Kennedy was assassinated, 22 November 1963 – **GERRY & THE PACEMAKERS** • *You'll Never Walk Alone*

TS Eliot died, 4 January 1965 – **THE BEATLES** • *I Feel Fine*

The *Torrey Canyon* disaster, 30 March 1967 – **ENGELBERT HUMPERDINCK** • *Release Me*

Radio 1 started, 30 September 1967 – **ENGELBERT HUMPERDINCK** • *The Last Waltz*

Concorde made its first test flight, 2 March 1969 – **PETER SARSTEDT** • *Where Do You Go To My Lovely*

Charles de Gaulle died, 9 November 1970 – **MATTHEWS SOUTHERN COMFORT** • *Woodstock*

Britain joined the EEC, 1 January 1973 – **LITTLE JIMMY OSMOND** • *Long-Haired Lover From Liverpool*

Noel Coward died, 26 March 1973 – **SLADE** • *Cum On Feel The Noize*

Agatha Christie died, 12 January 1976 – **QUEEN** • *Bohemian Rhapsody*

Margaret Thatcher won a second term as Prime Minister, 10 June 1982 –
   POLICE • *Every Breath You Take*

The space shuttle *Challenger* exploded on take off, 28 January 1986 – **A-HA**
   • *The Sun Always Shines on TV*

Massive storms raged across Britain, 16 October 1987 – **M/A/R/R/S** • *Pump
   Up The Volume*

Operation Desert Storm heralded the launch of the first Gulf War,
   17 January 1991 – **IRON MAIDEN** • *Bring Your Daughter To The Slaughter*

Tony Blair became leader of the Labour Party, 21 July 1994 – **WET, WET, WET**
   • *Love Is All Around*

pseud's

corner

Decca asked people to believe this wonderful piece of
nonsense in October 1965.

'Marc Bolan was born in September 1947. After fifteen
years had passed he travelled to Paris and met a black
magician called The Wizard. He lived for eighteen months
in The Wizard's château with Archimedes, an owl, and the
biggest, whitest Siamese cat you ever saw. He then felt the
need to spend some time alone so made his way to the
woods, near Rome. For two weeks he strove to find himself
and then returned to London, where he began to write.
His writings mirror his experiences with mentionings
of the magician's pact with the great god Pan.
In London, walking down King's Road, Chelsea
in the dead of night he chanced to meet a girl named
Lo-og who gave him a magic cat. This cat, named after
the girl, is now his constant companion and is a
source of inspiration to him.'

it's only bog 'n' roll

Flaxen-haired keyboard wizard Rick Wakeman was driving south over London's Hammersmith Bridge and along Castelnau when he was stopped by traffic police.

Having had a few and having recently got outside a particularly vicious curry, the Yes organist was racing home in order to deal with the particular functions needed to jettison an extremely hot vindaloo.

Being asked to step out of his car and blow into a Breathalyser was one hold-up too many. 'Look officer,' he pleaded, 'I'm on the brink of a very nasty accident,' and explained his predicament. The agreeable, but wary, constable accompanied him to the nearest house, but insisted on handcuffing him. This meant that while Rick was relaxing in the downstairs toilet of a compliant householder he was still handcuffed to the officer, whose arm was unnervingly some way inside the closet. Then a second arm appeared holding a pen and paper – it was the owner of the house. 'Ooohh, could you sign your name, Mr Wakeman?'

yes, no interlude

Rick Wakeman is the man who once said of his colleagues in Yes, 'They were going towards the cosmic stratosphere and I was going down the Dog and Duck.'

When he left the band in 1974 he did so under a bit of a cloud, or to be perfectly correct, a bit of a smell. One night at Manchester's Free Trade Hall, during the interminably long *Tales From Topographic Oceans*, Rick felt a little peckish and suggested to his roadie that a curry wouldn't go amiss. And not just a curry, but chicken vindaloo, Bombay aloo, bindi bhaji, stuffed paratha, pilau rice and six poppadoms.

Rick's roadie duly beat a path to a local curry house and no sooner was he away than he was back, by which time Yes were only up to side three of *Topographic Oceans*. At this point Rick's keyboards were not featuring and so he set about his Indian (having not expected it to arrive until after the show). Very quickly the rest of the band noticed the smell, and so, apparently, did the audience. At which point diminutive lead singer, Jon Anderson leans over the keyboard. 'Bloody hell, Rick. You've got a curry.' Rick's reply was equally to the point. 'I'm bored.'

Straight after the tour ended Rick left Yes, but he would be back . . . several times.

gentle man
not

Johnny Gentle, who once toured with the Beatles as his backing group, laid his former *nom de plume* to rest by making the following announcement of its demise:

GENTLE

On June 15 1962, At EMI Records Ltd,

JOHNNY GENTLE, aged 22 years.

No Mourning.

RIP

P.M.
tension

In the 1966 Eurovison Song Contest the Scandinavian countries all voted for each other and ignored the UK entry. One of their judges later confessed, 'It's because we are still very annoyed with your Mr Wilson [the then Prime Minister] and the import duty he placed on our goods going into your country, when we are supposed to be a free trade bloc with Britain.' Phew, what a relief, and there we were thinking that it was because Britain's entry, Kenneth McKeller's *A Man Without Love*, was totally out of step with what was happening in popular music!

keeping the faith

In the December 1987 issue of *Q* magazine Chris Heath reviewed *Faith*, George Michael's first album since Wham! had broken up a year or so earlier. George had already had solo success with *Careless Whisper* and *A Different Corner*, both of which had topped the UK singles chart. George had also reached No.1 earlier in 1987 in both the UK and the USA with *I Knew You Were Waiting*, a duet with Aretha Franklin. Everyone had great faith in George.

Mr Heath's intentions were clear from the start of his review. 'George Michael himself used to identify why Wham! were so successful. They had good songs of course, but beyond that they knew how to be pop stars.' After a short thesis on the Wham! story Mr Heath got to the nub of his gist. '*Faith* is, I fear, a reaction to Wham! and sadly in making it he seems to have thrown the baby (his songwriting talent) out with the bathwater (Wham!). Whatever the reason, it's an uneven, largely dull affair.' He then went on to rubbish every track on the album, even comparing George Michael to 'Shakin' Stevens on a good day', before closing with the immortal words, 'maybe he should have stuck with Andrew Ridgeley after all.' He rated the album as meriting two stars, which *Q* deemed 'poor'.

Faith, of course, was an enormous-selling album. It went to No.1 in Britain and spent 77 weeks on the charts. It spawned six UK hit singles, of which three went top 10. All this, though, pales when compared with George's success in America. *Faith* topped the album chart, sold over 10 million copies, won a Grammy as album of the year. It provided George with six hit singles, all of which went top 10 and four of which topped the US Hot 100. The album made George Michael a worldwide star.

Andrew Ridgeley divides his time between Monaco and Hertfordshire.

—— QUESTIONS DEMANDING AN ANSWER # 1 ——
**Can anyone spell Bjork's surname,
let alone pronounce it?**

steps to heaven

Years before his untimely death in 1961, Eddie Cochran had another brush with fate while on a hunting trip as a lad. His brother's .22 automatic jammed and while he was trying to work the lever, the gun went off and shot Eddie in the leg. The doctors successfully fought to save the limb, but Eddie had to spend several months in bed, during which time he decided to become a singer.

In October 1959 Eddie Cochran revealed, 'My fondest wish is to go to Britain.' He did so just a few months later and was killed in a car crash at Chippenham, Wiltshire, after appearing at Bristol. His friend Gene Vincent was with him and was injured.

At the time of the accident, he was being driven back to the airport and he was singing *California Here I Come*. One of the policemen who arrived at the scene of the accident was the young Dave Harman, who later became Dave Dee, leader of '60s hit act Dave Dee, Dozy, Beaky, Mick and Tich. In the immediate aftermath of the accident Dave became temporary custodian of Cochran's guitar.

which way you goin', billy?

You have to admire Sharon Osbourne. She not only manages husband Ozzy (is that an oxymoron?), but briefly for just four months in 2000 she performed the same task for the Smashing Pumpkins. Her resignation statement ranks up there with the best. It began, 'I must resign today due to medical reasons. Billy Corgan was making me sick.' It went on to accuse the Pumpkins' leader of other crimes against management. 'Billy's got an ego bigger than my arse,' said Sharon. For good measure Sharon threatened that if Corrigan said a bad word about her then 'her old man would chin him'. Her business acumen has been carefully honed over the years and was born out by her decision; the Pumpkins spent just one more week on the charts after the break up.

just
one more

At the tail end of a session to complete his album, singer Ralph McTell was eagerly looking forward to joining the musicians he'd been working with down at the pub. As he was about to leave, producer Gus Dudgeon asked him if he'd mind recording a song acoustically that he'd heard the singer strumming on occasions. McTell was unenthusiastic and said that he'd prefer to go down to the pub and forget about the song, as it was only a bit of fun and definitely not worth putting on the album. The persistent Dudgeon finally succeeded in wearing him down, and the reluctant singer laid down the song acoustically, but was still uncertain about the result. Gus Dudgeon's persistence paid off. The song, *Streets of London*, went on to become a No.2 in early 1975 and a perennial calling card for Ralph McTell for the following three decades.

a skin
full

As well as banging the skins, legendary drummer Phil Seaman also liked the odd tipple or two, strictly for medicinal purposes of course. On one occasion, when he was playing in the orchestra for the stage version of *The King And I*, a little imbibing and the warmth of the theatre led Phil to nod off. OK, perhaps, if there's not much going on, but as he dozed, a big percussive moment approached where he had to bang the gong to herald the entry of the king, played by Yul Brynner. The shaven-headed actor duly appeared on cue, but the hands of the slumbering drummer were hanging relaxed and limp by his sides. There was a silence, and an atmosphere that you could have cut with a knife. This lasted for a good twenty seconds until Seaman jolted awake and belatedly banged the gong. Without turning a hair, he looked at the audience, and, with the intonation and enunciation of someone who'd had a jolly good lunch, announced, 'Ladies and gentlemen, dinner is served.'

telephone bill

According to Bill Wyman, some time after he had left the Stones Charlie Watts called him one day from South America where his former band mates were touring and said. ''Ello Bill, it's Charlie.' 'Where are you?' asks Bill. 'Hang on. [Bill hears Charlie going to the other side of the room and then coming back. He picks up the phone again.] I'm in Buenos Aires. Anyway, Bill, tonight in the middle of the show I looked over to say something to you and you weren't there.'

be there **or** be square

Back in the Summer of Love, July 1967 to be precise, everyone was totally fascinated by flower power. *Disc and Music Echo* carried an ad inviting the public to a debate (admission 2 shillings) entitled 'Will Flower Power Work?' (in what terms they were unspecific). The Young Communist League, who organized the event, had thoughtfully booked the Conway Hall in Red Lion Square (near Holborn Tube) and cunningly called it not just a debate, but a 'Speak-In'. The ad ran just beneath a story about Paul McCartney's brother compering the International Love-In Festival at Alexandra Palace where 5,000 carnations would decorate the scene and Johnny Weider of Eric Burdon's Animals would play his electric violin for the first time in Britain.

you say **'allo** and I say **goodbye**

In 1963 a young man named Gordon Kaye interviewed the Beatles for a hospital radio station in Huddersfield. Gordon would eventually find fame as René Artois, the bar owner in TV's *'Allo 'Allo*.

I'm
a boy

The father of the Who's Pete Townshend was also a recording star. The Columbia Records hand-out for Cliff Townshend and His Singing Saxophone's version of *Unchained Melody* in June 1955 included the first-ever mention of the future driving force behind the Who. 'He [Cliff] is married and has a ten-year-old son called Peter.' Cliff Townshend was also a featured player with the Squadronaires, who had a 1953 hit called *Ricochet* with Joan Regan.

the
man with the
golden charm

When conductor/composer Elmer Bernstein joined up during the Second World War the US Army Air Force decided to direct his efforts into producing music for propaganda programmes and organizing music therapy schemes for the rehabilitation of operational fatigue victims.

able
kanes

The only three brothers to chart individually were the Indian-born Sarstedts. Big brother Richard became Eden Kane, Peter sang as Peter Sarstedt and little brother Clive became Robin Sarstedt. Eden and Peter had No.1s with *Well, I Ask You* and *Where Do You Go To My Lovely?* respectively, while Robin got to No.3 with *My Resistance Is Low*. They also recorded together in the mid-'60s, as the Brothers Kane.

rider saga

Nicky Wire of the Manic Street Preachers once said, 'If there aren't Golden Wonder salt and vinegar crisps in the dressing room I get a bit annoyed.' Nicky's needs, then, are comparatively simple. Not so some other bands' backstage requirements. It's the (Contract) Rider Saga.

THE RED HOT CHILI PEPPERS • a meditation room and aromatherapy candles

REEF • four pairs of socks (UK size 8–12) and four stamped local postcards

CHRISTINA AGUILERA • Oreo cookies and Flintstones vitamins

ORBITAL • mauve triple-ply toilet paper and no genetically modified anything

BRITNEY SPEARS • fresh tuna salad, Cool Ranch Doritos and Altoids breath mints

MOGWAI • a framed picture of Star Wars' Princess Leia.

DEF LEPPARD • specify that all leftover food is to be donated to a food centre for homeless

VAN HALEN • a bowl of M&Ms, but with all the brown ones taken out

KORN • a lawyer, doctor and dentist who are 'rock-friendly'

OZZY OSBOURNE • a vitamin B12 shot before shows

JAMES BROWN • an oxygen tank and mask on stage

Norwich's queen of nosh

Delia Smith baked and decorated the cake that appears on the cover of the Rolling Stones 1969 album *Let It Bleed*. 'I was working then as a jobbing home economist, with a food photographer who shot for commercials and magazines. I'd cook anything they needed. One day they said they wanted a cake for a Rolling Stones record cover. It was just another job at the time. They wanted it to be very over-the-top and as gaudy as I could make it!'

home
sales

Five of Simply Red's albums have topped the album charts and another two went top 10 so it must have been a surprise to everyone when Mick Hucknall's contract with Warners ended and he didn't re-sign with the label, or indeed any other major label. Instead he recorded his own album, in his own studio and then released it on his own label. It's cunningly titled *Home* and many of the sales have been through the internet – so far it's sold well over a million copies. Is this the shape of music sales to come?

— ONE LINER —

In 1979 Stephen Stills – of Crosby, Stills & Nash – became the first artist to record on digital equipment.

oh my **lord!**

Since the inception of the chart in November 1952, there have been only three charting hereditary lords.

The most successful was Lord David Dundas, who had a No.3 hit with *Jeans On* in 1976. Dundas was born David Paul Nicholas and is a member of one of the oldest families in Britain, Clan Dundas. It's said that any Prime Minister can raise a man to the House of Lords, but it takes seven centuries to make a 'Dundas of Dundas'.

Pop's second most successful peer of the realm is Old Etonian Charlie Brocket. Descended from the fifth-century King of Ulster, Niall of the Nine Hostages, Sir Charles Ronald George Nall-Cain became the 3rd Baron Brocket and is now Charlie Brocket, one third of the Jungle Boys, who had a top 30 hit in 2004 with *Jungle Rock*.

The third most successful hereditary peer, in chart terms, is Christopher Guest, alias Nigel Tufnell, lead guitarist of fictional pop group Spinal Tap, whose *Bitch School* made the top 40 in 1992. The film star and director, who is married to actress Jamie Lee Curtis, is now the 5th Baron Haden-Guest of Saling.

God
save **the** quinn

Before music publisher Ellis Rich had his own company he worked with EMI and one of his responsibilities was to copy the lyrics of songs that the company published. In copying out one of Bob Dylan's songs, he not unreasonably wrote down the title as *The Mighty Quinn*. The song was covered in the UK by Manfred Mann and subsequently entered the chart. So wasn't it a very happy Bob Dylan who happened to be in London and saw the song make a high new entry in the chart, heading towards No.1? No, not really,

He burst into the publishing office yelling, 'Which one of you assholes called my song *The Mighty Quinn*?' Ellis Rich tentatively put up his hand. It's *Quinn The Eskimo*!! Change it . . . now!' So the label copy was duly changed to *The Mighty Quinn (Quinn The Eskimo)*. Bob, however, was not appeased. In fact he was livid: 'That's *not* the title! It's *Quinn The Eskimo*, not *The Mighty Quinn (Quinn The Eskimo)*. Change it . . . now!'

So it became *Quinn The Eskimo (The Mighty Quinn)*. One might have thought that this too would have incurred more wrath from the poet formerly known as Robert Zimmerman, and although he wasn't exactly delighted, he let it go at that.

As well as playing with the Manfreds, lead singer on *The Mighty Quinn* (sorry, Bob) was Mike d'Abo who also fronts his own group, The Mighty Quintet. He's waiting with bated breath for Dylan to turn up at one of his gigs and yell, 'It should be Quinntet The Eskimo, asshole!'

not
so **miserable**

Before South African lyricist Herbert Kretzmer found fame and acclaim as the English lyricist to the musical *Les Miserables*, he had a career as a newspaperman and writer. One of his strangest assignments was to pen the lyrics to *Bangers and Mash* and *Goodness Gracious Me*, recorded by Peter Sellers and Sophia Loren in 1960. He wrote his homage to the great British sausage in the back of a car driving through France on his way to Spain.

In a publicity handout for the Bonzo Dog Doo Dah Band in 1966, Viv Stanshall claimed, 'I have burnished gold hair like an Arcadian shepherd boy', Roger Ruskin Spear listed his hobbies as 'house-breaking, shoplifting and homicide', and 'Legs' Larry Smith described his locks as being 'a delicate shade of autumn'.

— QUESTIONS DEMANDING AN ANSWER # 2 —
**Are the two bearded guys in ZZ Top
the same two guys who were there at the start,
or have they been replaced?**

the
name
game

Following the success of Belfast group Them, featuring Van Morrison, sneaky pop manager Reg Calvert, who futuristically specialized in lookalikes and soundalikes even back then and was not one to miss an opportunity, craftily registered the name Them Ltd in order to create another Them and cash in on something that, in reality, wasn't his. The real Them were managed by Dorothy Solomon, who was so incensed at this double-dealing that she played Calvert at his own game, registering two of his groups in her name. Calvert discovered that not only were the two in question his chart acts The Fortunes and Pinkerton's Assorted Colours, but that she'd bestowed the names on two unknown Birmingham groups whom she had signed to her own agency! The war heated up when an irate Calvert went for the jugular and Dorothy Solomon's biggest act by announcing, 'I am forming Bachelors Ltd.'

have a **cigar**

In the celebrity memorabilia stakes few items that
have come up for auction compare with Jim
Morrison's cigar humidor (at least that's how the
catalogue described it). It's estimated price was
£4,000–£5,000. Very rock 'n' roll.

rock **on wood**

Mickey Hart, who was once described as the 'semi-
legendary Grateful Dead drummer', published his
autobiography fifteen years ago. He insisted that his
publisher plant two trees for every one that had been
felled to make the book. For that he should be
elevated to legendary.

harmonic separation

What connects Level 42's 1987 top 10 single *It's
Over*, the theme tune from TV's *Last of The Summer
Wine*, the 1970 No.2 hit *Groovin' With Mr Bloe* and the
theme tune from TV's *Shoestring* detective drama?
One Harry Pitch played the harmonica on all of them.

$1 million, **that's** what's **so** good

Nick Lowe made a cool $1 million when his 1970 song *(What's So
Good 'Bout) Peace Love and Understanding* was covered by
Curtis Stigers and included on the soundtrack album of the
Whitney Houston film *The Bodyguard*. But it doesn't appear
anywhere in the movie.

royalty?

THE KING • Elvis Presley

KING OF THE BLUES • BB King had his first hit in 1951, and was still having them fifty years later

QUEEN OF SOUL • Aretha Franklin

BEN E. KING • Born a Nelson, he joined the Five Crowns who became the Drifters, by which time Benjamin was already a King

FREDDY KING AND ALBERT KING • Blues guitar legends who are no relation to the King of The Blues

EVELYN 'CHAMPAGNE' KING • Former cleaning lady turned disco diva

QUEEN LATIFAH • American rap star whose real name is Dana Owens

THE KINGS OF RHYTHM • Ike Turner's backing band in the '60s

THE RHYTHM KINGS • Bill Wyman's band after his retirement from the Rolling Stones

THE KING OF SWING • Clarinettist Benny Goodman

AUSTRALIA'S KING OF COUNTRY MUSIC • Slim Dusty

THE KING OF COUNTRY MUSIC • Roy Acuff, fiddle player and singer

THE QUEEN OF COUNTRY MUSIC • Kitty Wells or Reba McEntire, depending on who you believe

THE EMPRESS OF THE BLUES • Bessie Smith

KING OF RAGTIME • Scott Joplin

NAT 'KING' COLE • 'The Sepia Sinatra' who had over 100 American hits before he died aged forty-seven in 1965

KING • A British dance group from the '80s

CAROLE KING • The queen of singer/songwriters

REVD MARTIN LUTHER KING • An excerpt from his 'I have a dream' speech made No.88 in the American charts

KINGDOME COME • Arthur Brown's group after he left his Crazy World

KING CURTIS • Sax player who had hits in his own right and also led the Kingpins, the Queen of Soul's backing group

ROY ROGERS, THE KING OF THE COWBOYS

QUEEN • Topped the British singles chart six times

KING TUBBY • Former radio repairman Osbourne Ruddock who became a Reggae star

THE KING'S SINGERS • British group singing traditional songs who are probably unknown to every other king in this list

SAUNDERS KING • One of the first blues electric guitar players if not *the* first

KINGSIZE TAYLOR & THE DOMINOES • Liverpool contemporaries of the Beatles

PEE WEE KING • Singer and songwriter, his biggest hit: *The Tennessee Waltz*, his first: *Slow Poke*

THE KING OF SKIFFLE • Lonnie Donegan

WAYNE KING • The unintentionally funny '40s band leader

KING OF POP • Michael Jackson, definitely self-proclaimed

PRINCE • Who'll never be a king, no matter what

JONATHAN KING • Who cares?

TERRY, DRAG QUEEN OF THE BLUES • Probably self-proclaimed

i went
looking for a
jingle

In the early 1970s Alan Gordon, who co-wrote *Happy Together* for the Turtles, got a call asking him to compose a jingle. 'General Foods were testing a new product called Brrr, the world's first clear cola. A few days later I played the agency what I had come up with, "I went looking for a cola, a different kind of cola". They liked it and paid me a few hundred bucks, but informed me they were not going to put the product out.

'A month later I got a call asking me if I would write a spot for a new Ronzoni product called Country Kitchen Egg Noodles. I came up with, "I went looking for a noodle" – yep, the same song I used for Brrr! The ad agency loved it. I insisted on singing on the jingle – that's where you make the money – so I sang background on the session. Mr Ronzoni was at the session, with his nephew. I couldn't stop staring at him through the studio glass. I said to myself, "Look at this, here he is in the flesh: Mr Ronzoni." Boy, did he look great! I'll never forget what he was wearing. His shoes were as black and polished as an Italian black olive. He was wearing a dark blue pinstripe suit – but wait, they weren't pinstripes but thin linguini. His shirt was an off-white parmesan-colored silk affair. His designer tie had little rigatonis embroidered in silk, his golden tie clip was in the shape of an anchovy, and of course he had a beautiful olive complexion. The more I looked at him, the hungrier I got! When we finished, we all went to the control room. "How do you like it, Mr Ronzoni?" He forced a smile from his thin lips, then turned to his nephew and said something about me. I overheard the word "chemanide". I thought he was calling me a Stand Up Guy in Italian, and I said "Thank You Mr Ronzoni." When I drove back to Brooklyn, I went to my butcher Jimmy, and asked him what that word meant. He started to laugh and said, "LUNATIC DANCING FAIRY"!!!

'Anyway the jingle ran for a few years. I later rewrote the song and called it *I Found You Love*, which Barbra Streisand recorded on her *Superman* album. And, oh yes, the song started "I went looking for a new love", the same melody of course.'

i, me, mime

When Manfred Mann recorded *If You've Gotta Go, Go Now* at the Richmond Jazz & Blues Festival for the US TV show *Shindig*, Paul Jones happily sang the lyric 'or else you gotta stay all night'. This outrageous phrase was considered too risqué for the ears of young America, or indeed, any part of America, and the offending line was judiciously edited out. As US citizens gathered around their TV sets to enjoy the latest UK offering from the Manfreds, all they heard at that point was an ominous silence as Paul Jones's lips flapped gently in the wind.

Rory's rue

The Rock Gazetteer of France is probably not a volume that you're hankering after, but there is one place not to be missed. In Ris Orangis, a Paris suburb, is the Rue Rory Gallagher, named for the late Irish axeman after he performed in a local club. Not to be outdone Barking in Essex has a Bragg Close, named for Billy Bragg

rovers return

One of the earliest soap stars to land a recording contract was eighteen-year-old Jennifer Moss, who played Lucille Hewitt in *Coronation Street*. Her debut single, *Hobbies*, produced by Joe Meek, was released in June 1963, but despite *Corrie*'s weekly audience of 34 million, the single failed to chart. Although she didn't perform it on the series, the story line had her running away from home intent on becoming a pop singer. She was discovered hiding in an archway by the redoubtable Ena Sharples (Violet Carson), who sang Bryan Hyland's *Sealed With A Kiss* with her as a duet.

Proving his sense of humour held up to the end, Peter Sellers requested that Glenn Miller's _In The Mood_ be played as he was cremated.

the beat
svengali

Larry 'the Beat Svengali' Parnes was an old-fashioned manager of pop stars. He was dubbed 'Mr Parnes, Shillings and Pence', which gives you some idea of where Larry was coming from. Mr Parnes' theory of guaranteed stardom was simple; you needed a name that sounded right. Unlike Americans, whose real names always sounded right, postwar Britons were a plethora of Rons, Toms, Johns and even a few Clives. In fact Larry's inspiration was Rock Hudson, which probably tells you something more about Mr Parnes. Once a young hopeful was signed to Larry's 'stable of stars' he was quickly given a name that would look equally at home on a marquee and a Parlophone or Pye 45rpm single.

John Askew →	**Johnny Gentle**
Dave Nelson →	**Vince Eager**
Ray Howard →	**Duffy Power**
Richard Knellor →	**Dickie Pride**
Thomas Hicks →	**Tommy Steele**
Ronald Wycherley →	**Billy Fury**
Reginald Smith →	**Marty Wilde**
Clive Powell →	**Georgie Fame**

There were a very few who got away without a name change, including Peter Wynne. One young man was told he was going to be called Elmer Twitch, but somehow common sense prevailed and he stayed plain old Joe Brown.

— QUESTIONS DEMANDING AN ANSWER # 3 —
Have you wondered why you've never seen Jethro Tull and Channel 4's _Time Team_ presenters together in the same place?

fantasy
albums

No band have had their recordings covered more than the Beatles and you'd be surprised at the scope of the cover versions. Here are two Beatles albums made up entirely of genuine covers, and in the case of *Sgt Pepper* not one of them comes from the lamentable 1978 movie starring Peter Frarnpton and the Bee Gees.

Sgt Pepper's Lonely Hearts Club Band

SGT PEPPER'S LONELY HEARTS CLUB BAND • Physic TV
WITH A LITTLE HELP FROM MY FRIENDS • Herb Alpert & the Tijuana Brass
LUCY IN THE SKY WITH DIAMONDS • Noel Harrison
GETTING BETTER • Steve Hillage
FIXING A HOLE • Big Daddy
SHE'S LEAVING HOME • Baja Marimba Band
BEING FOR THE BENEFIT OF MR KITE • Frank Sidebotham
WITHIN YOU WITHOUT YOU • The Soulful Strings
WHEN I'M SIXTY-FOUR • Bernard Cribbins
LOVELY RITA • Fats Domino
GOOD MORNING, GOOD MORNING • Critical Mass
SGT PEPPER'S LONELY HEARTS CLUB BAND (REPRISE) • Jimi Hendrix
A DAY IN THE LIFE • Ipanema Beach Orchestra

Revolver

TAXMAN • The Bollock Brothers
ELEANOR RIGBY • Dr West's Medicine Show & Junk Band
I'M ONLY SLEEPING • Roseanne Cash
LOVE YOU TO • Bongwater
HERE, THERE & EVERYWHERE • Stephane Grapelli
YELLOW SUBMARINE • The Leningrad Cowboys
SHE SAID SHE SAID • Gov't Mule
GOOD DAY SUNSHINE • Jimmy James & The Vagabonds
AND YOUR BIRD CAN SING • The Flamin' Groovies
FOR NO ONE • Liza Minnelli
DOCTOR ROBERT • Bozo Allegro
I WANT TO TELL YOU • The Lambrettas
GOT TO GET YOU INTO MY LIFE • Sonny & Cher
TOMORROW NEVER KNOWS • The Grateful Dead

nudestock

In 1995 the first annual Nudestock festival took place in Michigan. Whereas at Woodstock and countless other festivals nudity was optional, at this one it was mandatory, but not for the bands. 'We're not paid to take our clothes off,' said Alan Parsons, whose Project was one of the headliners. Others on the bill included Foreigner and Kansas. The latter's Rich Williams, who remained clothed throughout, seemed to sum up the experience for everyone: 'And you're standing there playing and there's some guy with a baseball hat and tennis shoes standing in front of you, wiggling around and playing air guitar with his pecker. It bothers you.' The following year the organizers were hopeful of getting Oasis (the consequences could have been mind-boggling), Blur and Supergrass to participate, but they all declined. By the seventh Nudestock in 2004 the headliners were reduced to a Beatles tribute band and Tombstone Shadow, who were said to be more like Creedence Clearwater Revival than they were themselves.

all the young **nudes**

Following the demise of Mott The Hoople, front man Ian Hunter formed his own group and took them off to Canada to record in Montreal. In the middle of one particular night, when, surprisingly for a rock band, they were all fast asleep, the house in which they were living caught fire and subsequently exploded. A shivering Hunter and his men were stranded stark naked in the snow with the temperature reading four degrees below zero. Sadly, the Montreal press completely missed the most obvious headline, 'All The Young Nudes'.

up
creeque alley

Rolling Stones manager Andrew Loog Oldham was
so enamoured of the Mamas & Papas' single
California Dreamin' that, despite not having written,
produced or published the song, he took out a half-
page newspaper advertisement to extol its virtues.

California Dreamin' by the Mamas and Papas

Is more relevant today
Than the general election
Which can only bring more bigotry,
Unfulfilled promises
And the ultimately big bringdown.
California Dreamin' won't put the country back
    on its feet
But it will give you a helluva lift
For two minutes and thirty-two seconds
And sometimes that can be a long time.

He clearly thought the government was also up
Creeque Alley.

mills
and **boone**

In 1997 a US Christian TV network cancelled the show hosted by
the clean-cut, all-American family favourite Pat Boone. So what
dreadful crime had been committed by the religious sixty-three
year old – the great-great-great-great grandson of pioneer Daniel
Boone, a happily married man who once turned down a film role
starring with Marilyn Monroe because it would have meant kissing
a woman who wasn't his wife? The Florida-born singer had
appeared at the American Music awards in black leather and
sporting fake tattoos. Is nothing sacred?

stone me!

A new era for television was ushered in on 22 September 1955 when viewers in London were offered an alternative to the BBC. Associated Rediffusion and the Associated Broadcasting Company were commercial stations and carried advertising. Now we take for granted the fact that almost every advert has a music track to help sell the product. Back in the summer of 1955 British advertising agencies were just coming to terms with the concept. The first agency to record a piece of music specially for an ad was J. Walter Thompson on Monday 1 August 1955 when George Browne and his Calypso-Mambo Band recorded a one-minute song for use on a pilot commercial. In addition to George, who played the guitar and sang, the band members were Curly Clayton, also on guitar, and Pat Ryan on bongos. Seven years later, on 27 October 1962 – two weeks after the Beatles *Love Me Do* entered the charts – the fledgling Rolling Stones recorded three songs at Curly Clayton's studio near Arsenal's football ground in North London. The songs were made into a demo disc that was sent to EMI and Decca who, along with everyone else, rejected the band for a recording contract. However, in less than a year the Stones had signed for Decca Records and in early 1964 they recorded a song, in the style of Jimmy Reed, to be used in a TV advert for Rice Krispies. It too was made by J. Walter Thompson. In August 1995 Microsoft used the Rolling Stones *Start Me Up* to launch Windows '95. It paid an undisclosed sum to use this track, but you'd better believe it was a great deal more than the £400 that Kellogg's paid thirty-one years earlier. Curly, who is now living in Portugal, tells us he was paid £3 for that first session.

there's no such thing as a poor bookie

One of the enduring truisms of music journalism is that come each New Year the all-seeing editorial staff gaze into their crystal balls in an attempt to prophesy who'll make it big during the coming twelve months. So it stands to reason that the sense of anticipation built up at the dawn of a new decade is even more palpable. Naturally they don't always get it quite right, but few have got it so spectacularly wrong as the *Melody Maker* did back in 1970. They singled out twelve artists who, as they put it, 'this should be the year for'. They were Flock, Ginger Baker's Airforce, Rare Bird, Paul Rutherford, The Keith Tippett Band, Quintessence, The Pigsty Hill Light Orchestra, Jellybread, Ginny Richmond, Mighty Baby and Clarence Carter. These eleven acts managed two hit singles between them during the year and three hit albums, the most successful of which got to No.22. To spare the *Melody Maker* team's blushes, the final act tipped for stardom was Yes, who had did manage a (minor) hit album during 1970 (it got to No.45) and of course have been going reasonably strong ever since (most of the time, anyway). Having said that, the *MM* had also picked Yes in the same survey at the start of 1969.

turkey of the year

New Musical Express readers' votes for the 1976 Turkey of the Year Award.

1.	Sex Pistols	6.	Queen
2.	Johnny Rotten	7.	Peter Frampton
3.	Punk Rock	8.	Patti Smith
4.	Bay City Rollers	9.	Britt Ekland
5.	Bill Grundy	10.	Freddie Mercury

fancy licks

On the subject of riffs we know and love, what about young Chuck Berry – because he was young once. His 1958 classic *Johnny B. Goode* opened with an intro that has become something of a signature piece.

In actual fact, Chuck was playing under the influence. Twelve years earlier, in 1946, Louis Jordan was the man that every aspiring black musician looked up to. Along with his Tympany Five he recorded *Ain't That Just Like A Woman*. The guitarist with the Tympany Five was Carl Hogan and his guitar intro to the song was almost note-for-note the same as Chuck Berry's later recording. As the old adage goes, there ain't no such thing as new ideas, there's just old ones thought of again.

one day **at** a **time**

3 February 1959 was immortalized in the song *American Pie* by Don McLean as 'the day the music died'. It was the day on which Buddy Holly, Ritchie Valens and the Big Bopper died in a plane crash in Iowa.

On the same day eight years later Joe Meek, the eccentric, and sometimes brilliant, record producer, shot himself after shooting dead his landlady at his flat in the Holloway Road. Two years after that John, George and Ringo signed a management deal with Allen Klein, while Paul opted to go with his father-in-law, Lee Eastman. This was a year to the day after recording *Lady Madonna*, which was four years after they arrived in NYC to begin their first US tour. Two years to the day after Buddy Holly died Bob Dylan recorded his first song, *San Francisco Bay Blues*.

A number of rock and pop people have been born on 3 February. On the day Buddy died Lol Tolhurst of the Cure was born. In 1947 Dave Davies of the Kinks and Melanie were born. A year later Ozzy (although his mum called him John) Osbourne let out his first wail . . . and we'll refrain from making the obvious link.

at **No.10** it's Scott **walker,** at No.11 . . .

As Harold Wilson was winning a landslide victory in the 1966 General Election, *Disc* decided to hold its own poll to find out which pop star its readers would like to see as Prime Minister. Scott Walker was the clear winner, followed by John Lennon and Mick Jagger; another American came in fourth – P.J. Proby, he of the tight pants. You wonder who would have done what in the Cabinet.

Given Tony Blair's predilection to 'get out his guitar' and Bill Clinton's saxophonic talents, it seems that *Disc* may have been on to something.

is Steel heavy **metal?**

It's 1983 – a time long ago and well before Tony Blair even contemplated getting his guitar out for a jam in Downing Street. But David Steel, then leader of the Liberals, had pop pretensions of his own. He cut an utterly awful record called *I Feel Liberal – Alright* in an effort to appeal to the younger voters. The song was actually written and produced by Jesse Rae, the kilted rocker who lives near David Steel in the Scottish Borders. Rae had a minor hit in 1985 with *Over the Sea*. The cover of the Steel record illustrated the dance steps to *I Feel Liberal – Alright* but somehow you can't imagine anyone, even at an Lib disco, feeling suitably moved to get down and par-tee.

top of the polls

Politics and music have always had a strange relationship, and it's taken a new twist in the last decade as political parties have attempted to 'appeal to younger voters' by using pop music. The Labour Party used D-Ream's 1994 No.1 *Things Can Only Get Better* as the theme for their 1997 election campaign, when it was re-released and eased back into the top 20 at No.19. But often music has generally attacked the government of the day. It's an activity that goes back to the days of the blues and before. Few have done it more amusingly than the cast of Spitting Image who in 1984 updated the Phil Spector classic *Da Doo Ron Ron* as a song about Ronald Reagan's bid for re-election. (Two years later Spitting Image had a No.1 in Britain with *The Chicken Song* but this was in no way politically motivated.) It is probably fortunate for the Tories that Margaret Thatcher was not around when politics went pop: when asked to name her favourite song she unhesitatingly said *Telstar* by the Tornados (a massive hit in 1962). There seems to be no truth in the rumour that Tony Blair is so confident of victory at the next general election that he's asked the Bee Gees to re-record their 1987 No.1 *You Win Again* as *We'll Win Again*.

give 'em enough rope

In June 2004 it was reported that Tony Blair had once again started to play his guitar. Something about music and the troubled brow comes to mind, although his choice of songs puts that argument down. *Time Out* reported that he was playing Clash songs, an entirely appropriate choice given their back catalogue – *Complete Control*, *The Call Up* and, of course, *Should I Stay Or Should I Go*. However, the PM was not specific about which songs he favoured.

29

I'm telling you

Eddie Cochran's last record was, somewhat ironically, *Three Steps To Heaven*. After he was killed in April 1960 his label rushed it out and it climbed to No.1 in late June. But his prescience is nothing compared to that of Hank Williams whose record *I'll Never Get Out of This World Alive* entered the Country charts two weeks before he died from drug and alcohol abuse on New Year's Day 1953. It went on to be No.1, as did the three records that were released after the thirty-year-old country legend's demise.

word play

Record companies have a penchant for slogans that sell their wares. Phil Spector's Philles label had one of the best – 'Tomorrow's Sound Today', while Motown similarly captured the mood with 'The Sound Of Young America'. Andrew Loog Oldham came up with the line 'Happy To Be Part of The Industry of Human Happiness' when he started the Immediate label. But few have come close to matching CBS for absurdity. Anxious to appeal to the changing mood of the times in the late '60s its marketing gurus came up with 'The Revolutionaries are on CBS'.

no willy billy

Jazz saxophone legend Billy Tipton was very successful as a musician as well as having a lovely wife and three adopted boys. Even though Billy had been hanging out with the other guys in dressing rooms for all his playing life, it was only after his death that a funeral director in Spokane, Washington, revealed Mr Tipton was in fact a woman.

In 1966 *The Creation*, who had hits with *Painter Man* and *Making Time*, announced,
'We see our music as colours . . . it's purple with red flashes. CREATION 1 v. ii'

One critic, totally enamoured of the voice of Ethel Merman, wrote,
'She has the magnificent vitality of a steam calliope in red and gold coming down a circus midway.'

In 1966 Paul McCartney confessed,
'I wouldn't mind being a white-haired old man writing songs, but I'd hate to be a white-haired old Beatle.'

Earth-shattering headline featuring hot news about the Who's drummer from March 1966.
'Keith Moon Not To Wed'

With the emergence of punk, Queen's Freddie Mercury was asked what he thought of Sex Pistols front man Johnny Rotten, to which he replied,
'Johnny who, dear?'

Gene Vincent's last words were,
'If I get through this I'll be a better man.'

POP CRITIC KEITH FORDYCE REVIEWING CLIFF RICHARD'S *TRAVELLIN' LIGHT*:
'I'm doubtful about this platter reaching the very top.' Well, it was only No.1 for five weeks in 1959.

rob, bob and rod a job

What links Robert Mitchum, Bob Dylan and Rod Stewart? Marianne Faithful told an interviewer that all have tried and failed to have their wicked way with her.

mooning

Just after the Who's *Happy Jack* finishes you can hear Pete Townshend shout, 'I saw ya.' He's talking to Keith Moon, who had been such a pain during the band's attempts to sing the song that he had been banned from the vocal booth in the studio. Moon wanted to sing on the backing vocals and was creeping back to get in on the act.

boring santana

'Santana topped the US album charts in 1970 with *Abraxas* and it's difficult to see why. . . . They could be exciting if they weren't so boring.' The reviewer in *Disc* was clearly not a fan. *Abraxas* stayed on the UK album chart for a year and sealed the band's reputation.

berkeley . . . jane's harvest (well, her mother's)

A Nightingale Sang in Berkeley Square was written for Judy Campbell, the mother of '60s *enfant terrible* Jane Birkin. Birkin duetted with Serge Gainsberg on the No.1 hit *Je T'Aime, Moi Non Plus*.

the
NO greatest hits
tour

One Thursday afternoon in October 2001 Bill Wyman went to the basement of a small downtown shopping mall in Memphis; a blues festival was due to begin the next day. As he walked down the steps he heard the unmistakable sound of *Just a Little Bit*, a big hit for Roscoe Gordon in 1960. Bill was surprised to find Roscoe himself at the piano rehearsing with a small band. He asked Roscoe if he had missed the rehearsal for *Booted*, Gordon's classic R&B No.1 from 1952. 'Man, I don't play that song no more. In fact I ain't played it since 1953. I toured with BB King around the chittlin' circuit for six months and played that song six times every night. I got so fed up I ain't played it ever since.' Can you imagine another artist refusing to play their only chart-topper?

Roscoe was famous for what became known as 'Roscoe's Rhythm', as much a shuffle as it was a boogie, with elements of Jamaican Blue Beat about it. He died in 2002.

the **original**
potato man

Back in 1994 Peter Green had been absent from the musical scene for quite some time. His personal problems since leaving Fleetwood Mac had been well documented. An Essex farmer, known locally as 'the Egg & Potato Man', managed to convince a number of people that he was in fact the guitar legend. By all accounts he wasn't a bad player, especially when allowances were made for the man he was pretending to be's extended absence from the public eye. The farmer even spent time at the home of Queen's Roger Taylor where they discussed recording an album. In the end the only outcome of his stint in the limelight seemed to be that the man's business did well. 'We've sold a lot of potatoes and eggs because of all this,' he said after his little ruse was rumbled.

speculation

In 1995 Phil Spector began working with Celine Dion, but things fell apart after some of the tracks were finished and the working relationship ended. Mr Spector faxed *Entertainment Weekly* to complain that 'Celine's people' were the cause of the problems and not the singer herself. 'You don't tell Shakespeare what plays to write, you don't tell Mozart what operas to write and how to write them,' fumed Mr S. 'And you certainly don't tell Phil Spector what songs to write or how to write them, or what to produce or how to produce them.' So there.

grave
concern

The phrase *To Know Him Is To Love Him* was adapted from the inscription on Phil Spector's father's grave. It was also the title of the song that Phil wrote, produced and performed in 1958 with his group the Teddy Bears. Bruce Johnson, who later joined the Beach Boys, was asked along to the session to play bass but he declined because he had a date with a girl at his high school. Carol Conners, who was also in the Teddy Bears, later wrote *Gonna Fly Now*, the theme song to the movie *Rocky*.

spectacular

When the Ronettes first hit the big time a story did the rounds that Ronnie (real name Veronica) had phoned a friend and got the wrong number – the wrong number turned out to be Phil Spector. After chatting for a while he invited her and the Ronettes to audition. Unfortunately, like many great stories it was PR prattle. Ronnie's sister Estelle, who was also in the group had actually called Phil and he offered them an audition. They thought that they had done very well in persuading Phil to hear them but in fact he had seen them perform on a number of occasions and was anxious to meet Ronnie (who Phil later married). Somewhat appropriately their audition song was *Why Do Fools Fall In Love?*.

too much
information?

The wonderful world of fanzines forms an essential part of any music journalist's source material. There are literally thousands of self-published fan mags and the Beatles probably have more dedicated to their music than any other band or artist. In some cases fanzine editors seem to know more about the bands they write about than the bands do themselves. Some, like *Beach Boys Stomp*, have been going for decades, others last but an issue. Like tribute bands they have some wonderful names, many of which will only mean something if you're a real fan.

MORE BLACK THAN PURPLE • Ritchie Blackmore, Deep Purple guitarist
DARKER THAN BLUE • Deep Purple
BEACH BOYS • Beach Boys Stomp
ISIS • Bob Dylan
NOVA LEPIDOPTERA • Barclay James Harvest
BITS AND PIECES • Dave Clark Five
COLOURED RAIN • Traffic
SMILER • Rod Stewart
THE DAYS OF OUR LIVES • Queen
TIGHT BUT LOOSE • Led Zeppelin
UNSUGGED • Madness
JIMPRESS • Jimi Hendrix
THE CASTLE • Love
THE DARLINGS OF WAPPING WHARF LAUNDERETTE • The Small Faces
BROKEN ARROW • Neil Young
THE OFFICIAL MAGAZINE OF THE SUEDE INFORMATION SERVICE • does just what
    it says on the packet!
HOMEGROUND • Kate Bush
THE SLIDER • Marc Bolan
HERCULES • Elton John
SUZI AND OTHER FOUR LETTER WORDS • Suzi Quatro
SHATTERED • The Rolling Stones
DOG BYTES • Three Dog Night
NIGHTRAIN • Guns N'Roses
EDDIE'S • Iron Maiden
BLURB • Blur
COMA NATION • Porcupine Tree
BEATOLOGY • The Beatles
AFTER-MATH • Brian Jones
HOLDING TOGETHER • Jefferson Airplane
ESSENTIAL ELVIS
PAUL McCARTNEY.FM

the
economics
of dignity

It's well known, we think, that Deacon Blue took their
name from Steely Dan and they were similarly
inspired by the Dan to offer obscure references in
their songs. None more so than in *Dignity*, their first
hit record in 1988, which references Maynard
Keynes, the only known mention of the revered
economist and Bloomsbury group member to
appear in song. For that matter probably the only
reference ever made in song to any economist.

big in . . .

The biggest-selling record ever in Africa was *Sweet Mother* by
Nigerian Prince Nico and his Rocofil Jazz, which reportedly
shifted over 13 million copies after its release in 1976. *Nour el Ain
(You are the Light in My Eyes)* by Amr Diab, an Egyptian, was
recorded in 1996 and is the biggest-selling Arabic record ever.
She's So High by Kurt Nilsen became Norway's biggest-selling
single when it was released in 2003, going 11 times platinum.
Solo by Alsou, the Russian entry in the 2001 Eurovision Song
Contest, went on to become the country's biggest-selling record
of all time. *Local Boys* by Na Leo Pilimehana became the biggest-
selling record in Hawaiian history when it came out in 1984, and it
remains unbeaten; the three-girl harmony group are also 'big in
Japan'. Bic Runga's album *Beautiful Collision* became the
biggest-selling album ever by a local artist in New Zealand in
2003. Ruslana's album *Wild Dances* sold over 170,000 copies in
the Ukraine in 2002, making it the most successful official album
in the country's history – official because music piracy is rife and
few people buy the real thing. This makes measuring anything a
huge task in some countries. In states as diverse as Romania,
Bulgaria, China, Pakistan, Mexico, Brazil and Kenya piracy
accounts for well over 50 per cent of total sales.

stampede

It used to be big(ish) news when pop stars got themselves immortalized on a postage stamp. Certainly when the US Post Office used images of Frank Sinatra and Elvis Presley, stocks soon sold out. Jamaica even put Bob Marley on stamps commemorating his birth. Other countries soon cottoned on the fact that pop/rock+stamps meant big business. The former Soviet states of Kyrgyzstan, Tajikistan and Turkmenistan have turned the whole thing into a very lucrative overseas currency earner, because there are not too many home sales. Their stamps have featured all the usual suspects, including the Beatles, Abba, Mariah Carey, Queen and Madonna. Sometimes stamp designers have made some bizarre choices: Turkmenistan featured Peter Andre, Mali has stamped '60s US 'heart throb' Fabian, and Sting is big in the Belgian Congo, while Grenada issued a set of stamps a few years ago with paintings that are so bad they bear little more than a passing resemblance to a wide-ranging group of artists including Cher, Dolly Parton, Johnny Mathis and Janis Joplin. Somewhat against the odds, in June 2003 Austria became the first country to issue stamps featuring the Rolling Stones.

gypsy woman

Lou Christie, purveyor of such hits as *Lightnin' Strikes* and *I'm Gonna Make You Mine*, wrote all his songs with Twyla Herbert, a female clairvoyant twenty years his senior. She claimed that she could predict his hit records. Her uncanny power failed to extend beyond 1969 in the United Kingdom and 1974 in the States.

— ONE-LINER —
Growing up in Nairobi, Roger Whittaker spoke Swahili before he learned to speak English.
(But he always whistled in English)

carriage
mystery

Some songs seem to have an almost mystical power for musicians of a certain age. One such is *Mystery Train*. It was first recorded in late 1953 by a band led by Herman Parker, better known as Little Junior Parker. He did it for Sam Phillips' Sun Records.

'When Elvis came in I found out that *Mystery Train* was so embedded in Elvis's mind that when he started to sing it, it was a natural as breathing,' said Sam. Elvis cut *Mystery Train* in July 1955, a year and a few days after his first session in Sun's studio at 706 Union Avenue, Memphis. You can hear Elvis laugh at the end of the record; he did not think it was a take. It became Presley's last Sun single but failed to make either the *Billboard* chart or the R&B chart. It did, however, make No.11 on the Country chart in September 1955.

The lyrical inspiration for *Mystery Train* came from a song that both black and white people throughout the South knew very well. The song, first recorded by the Carter Family in 1930 as *Worried Man Blues*, had the lines 'The train I ride is sixteen coaches long, the girl I love is on that train and gone'. On a 1944 recording Woody Guthrie added five coaches. Then in October 1955, a few weeks after Elvis's *Mystery Train* charted in America, Lonnie Donegan recorded *Worried Man Blues*; he decided that twenty-one was the right number of coaches for him too. Little Junior Parker stuck to sixteen coaches but the Grateful Dead, who performed the song just once at a live concert in 1970, chose to reduce the number of carriages to fifteen. Who knows why.

legends all

While former beatnik Rod Stewart, with a massive forty-eight weeks on the listings, was the most successful singles artist of 1976, the least successful, with just one week each on the chart, were recording legends Frank Sinatra, Johnny Cash, Hall & Oates and the Wombles.

Twice As Much singer David Skinner, who with partner Andrew Rose had a hit with *Sittin' on a Fence*, was written up by the publicity maestros as spending 'much of his time painting in a vague aura of surrealism and pointillism. Or listening to Bach or Debussy. David is a quiet person with a wish to be happy. But it will be hard. For David is that introspective person you see, who looks and knows. And people that know are seldom happy.' He later toured with Roxy Music as their keyboard player. What does that tell you?

chukka khan?

The proof that royal and musical circles were getting closer was born out in 1966 when *White Christmas* crooner and part-time golfer Bing Crosby invited Prince Philip to take part in a charity polo match at Palm Desert, California. He obviously wanted a pukka chukka mucker.

very confused

Sixties folkie Jake Holmes had originally been around the New York scene in a group with Tim Rose before they both went solo. Holmes wrote the original version of *Dazed and Confused* and it appeared on his 1967 debut album. He opened for the Yardbirds, who included Jimmy Page, at a club in New York City. The Yardbirds started doing *Dazed and Confused* in their live shows and later Led Zeppelin covered it on their first album, but for reasons that are not altogether clear it was credited to just Jimmy Page.

Holmes later made a career writing advertising jingles. His best known are 'Be All You Can Be' for the US Army, 'Raise Your Hand If You're Sure' for Sure deodorant, and the 'Be A Pepper' for Dr Pepper.

thirty-four
years on

Back in the autumn of 1970 Elton John was hardly a household name. He hadn't even had a hit single, although his debut album had just failed to make the top 10. He had just returned from a trip to the USA with his writing partner Bernie Taupin, a trip intended to sell their songs as much as to sell 'Elton the singer'. After getting back to the UK the artist formerly known as Reg let out his innermost thoughts: 'In America everyone gets over-excited and I found I had to take a few people doing my promotion aside and tell them to calm down. Imagine how I felt being introduced to Leon Russell as Elton John – Superstar. I suppose it's because I'm basically very quiet that I don't revel in that kind of thing. I hate it when things get blown out of all proportion.'

that's
entertainment

If you were living in London in February 1970 your opportunities to hear great live music were unrivalled. On Friday 27th you could take a little trip by tube out to Uxbridge to Brunel University and catch Fairport Convention. A new band called Genesis were supporting them. Saturday night and you're Essex-bound to the Basildon Arts Workshop for one of the very first gigs by 'David Bowie's new electric band' (called that because they still hadn't got a name, according to the advert). Sunday and it's the Lyceum in the Strand for the first London appearance by the Faces. Monday is always a slow night but the Groundhogs are at Richmond Athletic Club. Tuesday and Love along with Blodwyn Pig play London's Imperial College, and if you don't fancy that, Mississippi Fred McDowell is at the 100 Club in Oxford Street. Wednesday it's Taste in Tooting and Thursday it's Caravan at the Marquee. To round off the week Pink Floyd and Juicy Lucy play Imperial Collage, and if you have the stamina there's an all-nighter at the Lyceum with Keef Hartley's Big Band, The Crazy World of Arthur Brown, Free and East of Eden.

you're not quite right for us

Visit any A&R man's office – if you can get in through the piles of tapes, CDs and assorted garbage – and you'll find a beleaguered man. Bombarded with demos from eager hopefuls, Mr A&R is charged with trying to try to sort the wheat from the chaff. Every artist who has made it – and every artist who hasn't – has a demo tape story, but two stand out. One band were so frustrated by the whole process that they submitted a tape of Steely Dan tracks to an A&R man; needless to say, they got the rejection letter. American rock giants Boston submitted a tape to dozens of record companies in America over a period of years. Most didn't even bother to respond but the likes of Atlantic, Warner Brothers, RCA and Epic all rejected them. Boston decided their approach must be all wrong; they became involved with some industry heavyweights who resubmitted the same tape. Within the time taken for a CD to make just one revolution they were signed to Epic. The material became their first album, *Boston*, and went on to sell 16 million copies. It's not what you know . . .

telephone line

ELO's first album came out in the UK in December 1971 and featured not just Jeff Lynne but his fellow band mates from the Move, Roy Wood and Bev Beven. Indeed it's often been claimed that the whole idea for this Move offshoot was pretty much Wood's. However, what's fascinating about ELO's debut, imaginatively titled *The Electric Light Orchestra* in Britain, is its American release. The head of the US label was trying to get information prior to the record being pressed and released in America and got his secretary to call the London office to find out what the album was called. The secretary couldn't get through so she left a note for her boss, which is how ELO's album came to be called *No Answer* in America.

have you **guessed** what **it is** **yet?**

A very early publicity handout for the up-and-coming chart artist and wobbleboard expert Rolf Harris proclaimed: 'It's a fair bet that ten years from now, people will recall that it was early in this decade that wobbleboards caught on . . . bearded 26-year-old Rolf uses it to accompany himself on his first recording to be issued in this country, *Tie Me Kangaroo Down Sport*. . . . To make a genuine, class-one wobbleboard, take one piece of building board (or cardboard will do) about three feet long and eighteen inches wide, grasp it firmly at both ends and with a flick of the wrists bend it up and down. Appropriate noises ("w-h-o-o-l-p" and "b-e-l-o-o-p") will immediately be forthcoming. If you want to be like Rolf Harris and at the same time be one up on your wobbleboarding neighbours, a portrait painted on the wobbleboard is recommended.'

hyperbole

Now everyone knows music is a business that lends itself to going over the top. But in recent times few can have been quite as effusive as John Peel, who is, after all, not known for it. He commented thus on Laura Cantrell's 2000 debut album *Not The Tremblin Kind*: 'My favourite record of the last ten years and possibly my life.' You'll be forgiven if you say you're not familiar with it because it didn't set the sales tills alight.

latvian leviathan

If ever you doubted that Take That were truly an international band, take note: they topped the Latvian airplay charts in 1995 with *Back For Good*.

insider
training

The Somerset-born Acker Bilk, who had phenomenal success with *Stranger on the Shore*, took up the clarinet during his time in an army prison camp. He had been given three months for falling asleep on guard duty and while inside he asked for a clarinet to pass the time.

— QUESTIONS DEMANDING AN ANSWER # 4 —

How do you go from being a member of the Incredible String Band to mayor of Aberystwyth like Rose Simpson did?

you spin me round (like a record)

At the beginning of 1949, in answer to Columbia's new 33⅓ discs of the previous year, RCA Victor introduced 45rpm records. Determined not to let the small discs slip away after just twelve months, RCA spent a massive $5 million on promoting 45rpm records as the public's preferred speed. A key player in RCA Victor's plan was to be Arthur Crudup – his *That's All Right* became the first 45rpm single in Victor's R&B series. Some dynamic marketing executive had the idea of colour coding the RCA releases. *That's All Right* came out on orange vinyl, popular music on blue, country records, rather appropriately, were green. Though *That's All Right* did get some airplay on black radio stations, it failed to chart. However, RCA's plan worked and the single became a pivotal part of the collection of all young record buyers growing up in the '50s, '60s, '70s and '80s. At the beginning of 1949, in answer to Columbia's new 33⅓ discs of the previous year, RCA Victor introduced 45rpm records. By the end of the year, however, it looked as though RCA's invention was to be short-lived and would be permanently supplanted by the other speed.

big **business**
meets
show business

Back in the 1950s the popularity of the blues was unrivalled in Memphis, with BB King, Howlin' Wolf, Sonny Boy Williamson, Little Junior Parker, and Bobby Bland just some of the great musicians playing around the town and across the Mississippi in West Memphis. Sonny Boy was *the* man, and when he gave up the residency of a West Memphis club there was fierce competition to get his gig.

The owner decided to have a competition at which various artists got to play and the best audience reaction would secure the gig. BB King was there and tells the story better than I can.

'Everybody had been on stage and Little Milton and myself, you know, we do what we do but we couldn't move the crowd quickly like Bobby Bland. We had all been on and now Howlin' Wolf is up and the people are going crazy man. So I said to Little Milton, "Now I know Bobby Bland is good, the girls just go crazy," and Milton say, "Yes, but something is going on out there." Junior Parker says, "Let's check it out." So out we go and Wolf is doing *Spoonful*, and he's on his knees crawling round on the floor. The people are just going crazy. His pants was busted, the seat of his pants was busted! And all of his business is hanging out!'

— SOUNDBITE —
'Howlin' Wolf? . . . I've never heard of him.'
DESMOND DEKKER, *Bluebeat star*

— SOUNDBITE —
**'So what's the use of getting sober,
when you're gonna get drunk again?'**
LOUIS JORDAN 1942

blues **law**

Many Americans seem fascinated by the fact that the British are fascinated by the blues. But our passion is hardly surprising when you know that it was a 34-year-old British born A&R man for ARC Records who 'discovered' Robert Johnson. The Delta bluesman had gone to San Antonio to be recorded by the label in November 1936 and Don Law, an Englishman, produced the session. He had emigrated to the USA in 1924, aged twenty-two, from the capital where he was a member of the London Choral Society. Law later worked for Columbia in the country music division with artists like Marty Robbins.

the
irish blues
boy

BB King has the most famous initials in the blues, and probably in all music. This is his account of how his name came about.

'When I was a disc jockey at the beginning, they used to bill me as Blues Boy, the boy from Beale Street. When people would write me, instead of saying the Blues Boy, they'd just abbreviate it to BB. But my name is Riley B. King. When I was in Ireland I was telling the people over there that I guess I feel a little Irish because I was born on this plantation and my dad worked for a person named Jim O'Riley. He and my dad were such good friends that they named me after him, but left the O off. So when I got big enough to know about it, I asked my dad one day. I said, "Dad, why is it that you named me after Mr O'Riley, why did you leave the O off?" He said, "You didn't look Irish enough!"

'Anyway the B is just a middle initial. In the south, especially Mississippi, Alabama, Georgia, you find a lot of people with just initials for a name. I know a person named E.H. Hemphill and that's all I know, E.H. Hemphill. I was at school with him and he's just called E.H.'

bart & the guys

Early in the summer of 1958 a young Cliff Richard (or Harry Webb as he was then), asked songwriter Lionel Bart to come and hear his group and offer some advice. On the day, the seventeen-year-old and his friends waited keenly and nervously for the great writer to arrive. This was a big deal, after all he'd written songs for Tommy Steele! Bart duly arrived at the house in Cheshunt to be confronted by a clutch of spotty teenagers. He recalled the day vividly: 'The group set up their gear in Cliff's front room and we tried out dozens of numbers. They were good, but in the end I had to advise them against continuing with their idea of entering show business.' Good call, Lionel!

that seals it then, seal

Seal gave eponymous a whole new meaning with the release of his third CD in 2003. It was called *Seal*, and, you've guessed it, so were his previous two albums. It makes Chicago seem like a band with wit and imagination.

glad to be here

Unlikely hit pianist Mrs Mills ('Call me "Glad". Everyone else does.') was spotted at Woodford Golf Club and within weeks found herself appearing on the top-rated TV programme, *The Billy Cotton Band Show*. EMI then released her first single, *Mrs Mills Medley* (1961), while she was still superintendent of the typing department at the Paymaster-General's Office in London. A 'flabbergasted and overwhelmed Gladys Mills' admitted that success was something of a surprise as she was in her mid-forties and just under 16 stones.

minimum
wage

Woodstock's best-paid artists: Jimi Hendrix $18,000, Blood Sweat & Tears $15,000, the Who $12,500, Creedence Clearwater Revival $10,000, Joan Baez $10,000, making her the second highest paid individual. The lowest paid were Quill, the opening act on day two; they got just $350. On a man-for-man basis Santana came off worst – they got just $750 to split between all of them.

oh
hippy days

The Bickershaw Festival in 1972. What do you mean you've never heard of it? It was Britain's answer to Woodstock. The only problem was it took place a few miles from Wigan in Lancashire and unfortunately it was in May, which means, of course, that it rained. And it was staged next to a working coal mine. The headliners on the three consecutive evenings were Dr John, Captain Beefheart and his Magic Band, and the Grateful Dead. Leading the British contingent were Hawkwind (inevitably), Wishbone Ash, Family and Donovan. To cap it all, the festival organizer was Jeremy Beadle.

memories
of a
free festival

The first free concert to be held in London's Hyde Park took place on 29 June 1968. Topping the bill were Pink Floyd, supported by Jethro Tull (they even had their name on the drum kit), Tyrannosaurus Rex and the ubiquitous Roy Harper. The stage was open on all four sides.

messin'
with mahesh

To name the most unsuccessful tour of all time is perhaps difficult, as the criteria could be open to some debate. But certainly the Beach Boys US tour in May 1968 would probably win the award for the least successful tour by a major band. While admittedly the band's fortunes had slipped slightly since the heady days of December 1966 when *Good Vibrations* went to No.1 in America, they were still very popular. The band had become involved with the Maharishi Mahesh Yogi, particularly after Mike Love visited India in early 1968 along with the Beatles. After Mike returned he wrote and the band recorded *Transcendental Meditation* in April. A tour of seventeen cities was organized, with the Maharishi as the Beach Boys' 'opening act'.

Unfortunately anyone who bothered to attend the gigs quickly got bored with what the great man had to say while seated on a stage surrounded by masses of flowers. Catcalls are said to have drowned out most of his words. Pretty soon the MMY found he had a better offer, a movie contract. He jumped ship and the Beach Boys cancelled the rest of the shows. According to Al Jardine, 'If anybody benefits from this tour it will be florists.' In fact the Beach Boys are said to have lost around $500,000, somewhere between $5–6 million today. It marked a turning point in the band's career: shortly after the tour their new album, *Friends* (which included *Transcendental Meditation*) could only stagger to No.126 in the *Billboard* chart. While it did make No.13 in Britain, in America things were never quite the same for the band. It would be another eight years before they again had an American top 10 single, *Rock and Roll Music*.

(you're my) **soul** and **inspiration**

Pattie Boyd (once Mrs George Harrison and later Mrs Eric Clapton) must hold the record for inspiring the most songs about the same person.

SOMETHING • The Beatles
I NEED YOU • The Beatles
FOR YOU BLUE • The Beatles
SO SAD • George Harrison
LAYLA • Derek & The Dominoes
WONDERFUL TONIGHT • Eric Clapton
THE SHAPE YOU'RE IN • Eric Clapton
PRETTY GIRL • Eric Clapton
MAN IN LOVE • Eric Clapton

sign here

Beatles publisher Dick James worked as a barber and then as a gentlemen's outfitter before singing with several bands. Among the famous orchestras and bands with which he appeared were Henry Hall and Geraldo. In 1956 he had hits with children's favourites *Robin Hood* and *The Ballad of Davy Crockett*, before signing the Beatles to their first publishing deal with his new company in January 1963.

I'll be **back**

From 1943, double-chart-topping singer and '50s legend Dickie Valentine was the call-boy at the Palace Theatre, Manchester, Her Majesty's Theatre and the London Palladium. He was actually sacked by the Palladium for being cheeky to the head commissionaire. In 1954 he would return to the place from which he was ignominiously fired to top the bill.

brief encounter

Tom Jones has admitted that although he is more than happy for knickers to be thrown during his raunchier songs, he doesn't appreciate it during slower numbers. 'When I'm singing a ballad and a pair of knickers lands on my head, I hate that. . . . It really spoils the mood.' Jones the Voice also has a grievance against unworn knickers coming his way, 'Normally they bring along a plastic bag with the underwear in. It has nothing to do with enthusiasm anymore. I give it my all on stage 'cause I want to fill the crowd with enthusiasm, but that comes from the heart, not from a plastic bag!'

take me to the pilot

Bruce Dickinson joined Iron Maiden in late 1981. He played his first gig in Italy after driving thirty-six hours in a van to get there. He can scarcely have imagined that twenty years later he would be flying to the Mediterranean, and not as a passenger, but piloting a Boeing 737 as a first officer on British charter airline Astreus. After enjoying twelve years with Iron Maiden Bruce left in 1993, citing the inevitable musical differences. Bruce pursued a solo career and took up flying seriously, gaining his commercial pilot's licence. He did get back with Maiden in 1999 but not before he began flying for an airline. After a flight he was in uniform in Munich airport and was accosted by a German Iron Maiden fan in full battle dress (tour T-shirt, cross, etc). 'Hello? But I must know . . . Is this the bus to Munich?' The Maiden reunion spawned a number of hits including *Wicker Man*, which meant that Bruce was the first airline pilot to have a top 10 record on the UK singles chart.

maiden's
under
garments

Everyone knows that ladies of a certain age have, in the past, offered articles of underwear to singers of a certain age while they are performing on stage. Not everyone will know that it was something actively encouraged by Iron Maiden during the heady days of the '80s. They were known to play requests written on said garments during the band's encores. Two Iron Maiden fans from Bookham in Surrey went to a gig in 1985 at the Hammersmith Odeon determined to have their favourite played. Prior to the gig it was clear that there was one obvious flaw in the plan: a ready source of ladies' panties. Being aged fifteen, and not too well acquainted with any females, they were somewhat stumped. Thoughts of nicking a pair of their mothers' knickers were quickly rejected as unsuitable on all levels. Then one of them hit on a master-stroke. He got a pair of his (washed) Y fronts and wrote 'Charlotte was here' on them. At the appropriate moment he lobbed them on to the stage from his fourth-row seat (although they weighed enough to have made it from the back of the theatre). Bruce Dickinson rather gamely picked them up, triumphantly held them aloft and read out the note before Maiden launched into *22 Acacia Avenue*, with lyrics about 'Charlotte the harlot'. Life in Bookham would never be the same again.

justin case

Lonnie Donegan was fond of telling people how badly done by he was over the recording of his debut hit, *Rock Island Line*, in 1956. He had received the standard session fee of £3.50, which worked out at 70p per song for the five he cut that day. He didn't receive any money in royalties when *Rock Island Line* sold 3 million copies in six months.

But Lonnie wasn't always so hard done by. In 1965 he signed a nineteen-year-old singer named Justin Hayward to a management and publishing contract with his Tyler Music Company. Justin had been in Marty Wilde's group and after signing with Lonnie he released a single on Pye and then another on Parlophone. In 1966 Justin joined the Moody Blues and soon began work on their ground-breaking *Days of Future Passed* album. The biggest hit from that album was *Nights in White Satin*, which has charted in Britain three times and reached No.2 on the US Hot 100. The song is published by Tyler Music, Lonnie's company, and earned the King of Skiffle a veritable fortune over the years. And it wasn't just that song. Most of Justin's other songs that featured on the Moody Blues' million-selling albums were published by Tyler Music too. Justin apparently tried unsuccessfully to 'buy back' his songs on a number of occasions before Lonnie died in 2002.

shafted

In 1976 the National Coal Board got Max Bygraves to record *Do It The Safety Way* to encourage better pit safety; naturally the Grimethorpe Colliery Band provided the accompaniment. Why the NCB settled on Max is anyone's guess but it's rather a shame they stopped at just a single and didn't go for the whole shebang. Max could have lent his unique vocal talents to Lee Dorsey's *Working in a Coal Mine*, Jerry Reed's *She Got The Goldmine (I Got the Shaft)*, Lou Christie's *Gonna Make You Mine* and many others. Although good taste would have prevented his covering the Bee Gees' *New York Mining Disaster 1941*.

hirsute suits you, sir

Ten stars who once sported beards

> Frank Sinatra
> Elvis
> David Bowie
> Bono
> Sir Mick Jagger
> Sir Elton John
> Sir Cliff Richard
> Phil Collins
> David Essex
> Sir Paul McCartney
> *Then there's* Frank Beard of ZZ Top,
> *who doesn't have one.*

argie-bargie

Tanglewood was a semi-pro band from Kent. One Saturday night in early May 1982, during the Falklands War, they were booked into an ex-servicemen's club in London. Their then drummer, Jez Yates-Round, takes up the story. 'Unfortunately our bass player was ill and we had to get a guy called Neil from Essex to dep for him. Things started off well and we had just begun playing our signature cover of Creedence Clearwater's *Bad Moon Rising* when two guys from the audience dragged Neil the bass from the stage and started to beat him up. Neil had very dark hair, was tanned and had a droopy moustache, which for some reason gave these two the notion that he was an Argentinean. We called it a night after we'd rescued Neil.'

— SOUNDBITE —

No need ever to have to sum up the United States in one line, as John Denver had that one covered.

'I epitomize America,' he said.

ten artists who had
No.1 albums in Britain
then released a follow-up that was barely noticed

ACE OF BASS • *Happy Nation*, 1994 ➙ *The Bridge*, No.66 in 1995

PETER ANDRE • *Natural*, 1996 ➙ *Time*, No.28 in 1997

TRACY CHAPMAN • *Crossroads*, 1989 ➙ *Matter of the Heart*, No.19 in 1992

CHAKA DEMUS AND PLIERS • *Tease Me*, 1994 ➙ *She Don't Let Nobody*, failed to chart in 1995

ERASURE • *I Say, I Say, I Say*, 1994 ➙ *Erasure*, No.14 in 1995

THE FARM • *Spartacus*, 1991 ➙ *Love See No Colour*, failed to chart in 1992

HOLLY JOHNSON • *Blast*, 1989 ➙ *Dreams That Money Can't Buy*, failed to chart in 1992

KULA SHAKER • *,K*, (1996) ➙ *Peasants, Pigs & Astronauts*, No.10 in 1999

RIGHT SAID FRED • *Up*, 1992 ➙ *Sex and Travel*, No.35 in 1993

TRANSVISION VAMP • *Velveteen*, 1989 ➙ *Little Magnets vs The Big Bubble of Babble*, failed to chart in 1991

the **long**
& the **short**

39 minutes 58 seconds was the running time of the Orb's 1992 single *Blue Room*, which reached No.8. It was two seconds shorter than the maximum permitted length of a single to be considered for the charts. To think that in the '60s the industry used to get excited by a single of over 7 minutes. The shortest single to top the charts was Adam Faith's *What Do You Want* in 1959; it ran for 1 minute 38 seconds.

first among
many

The first Lennon & McCartney song to make the *Billboard* charts was Del Shannon's *From Me To You* (it made No.77) on 29 June 1963. It was 18 January 1964 when the Beatles *I Want To Hold Your Hand* first charted in the US.

fantasy
festival

Each year festivals seem to become more eclectic in their line up (at Glastonbury in 2004 there were both Macca and the English National Opera among a diverse array of talent). Might it be better to theme each day's running order? We offer you:

Jon Hiseman's Coliseum
Nero & The Gladiators
Roman Holliday

Little Caesar & The Romans

Adrian's Wall

Special guest Lionel Richie

Compere Sid Caesar

The Lemonheads
The Black Grapes
Bananarama

Apples in Stereo

Strawberry Alarm Clock

The Raspberries

Orange

With special guest – Nick Berry

God
Jesus Jones
Madonna

Judas Priest

The Mission

The Lords of The New Church

By special arrangement – Shane MacGowan & The Popes

The Acoustic
Tent

The Presidents of the United States of America,
Bush and Ice Cube featuring George Clinton

hallowed
ground

Elvis Presley spent just one hour in the UK. It was at
Prestwick Airport in Ayrshire, Scotland. On 2 March
1960 his aircraft was refuelling en-route from
Germany to the USA. Elvis was on the way home
after finishing his national service in the US Army.

when **bobby** met **teddy**

Speaking on *Any Questions* at the time of Bill Haley and *Rock Around the Clock* (the movie was released in 1956), Bob Boothby, later Lord Boothby, commented: 'It's not my idea of fun at all. And I think that one of the purposes in life for us old fogeys is to stop young people from being silly. And they're being exceptionally silly. There are better things to do in life and much more fun to be had than jiving. And if they cause a lot of trouble and row in cinemas and upset people and if they want to be teddy-bears [sic] . . . well, I'd rather they go off to Cairo [this was during the Suez crisis] and start teddy-boying around there. As soon as this ridiculous film is banned altogether the better; it's causing a lot of trouble to a lot of people and giving no pleasure except to a few harmless but quite irresponsible lunatics.'

temporary flame

It's perhaps hard to imagine, or even remember, that back in the early '70s Slade were enormous. Starting with *Coz I Love You* they had a run of twelve huge hits between October 1971 and December 1974. Every one made the top 4 and six of them got to No.1. So how come their only movie was such a flop? They starred in *Flame* along with Tom Conti in 1974 and today hardly anyone can recall it. Maybe it's just as well.

finger-**clicking** good

'This is the boy who always reminds me of Anthony Newley. And he writes his own material too. A tongue in cheek lyric sung with a chuckle in the voice and swept along by a colourful and imaginative scoring and a thunderous finger-clicking beat. There's also a cute la-la chorus, a few side comments and a "hearts and flowers" finale. A disc with a difference.' So said a review of David Bowie's 1967 single *Love You 'Till Tuesday*, his sixth release after his 1966 debut. It would be over two years before David Bowie finally cracked the charts with *Space Oddity*.

hello children everywhere

Back in 1954 the BBC Light Programme started a show called *Children's Favourites* presented by Uncle Mac (real name Derek McCulloch). Every show began with the immortal words 'Hello children everywhere', spoken over the theme song, *Puffing Billy*. The show was built around genuine requests from the show's audience. Some weeks thousands of requests on a postcard ('50s email) were received for songs like Max Bygraves' *You're a Pink Toothbrush, I'm A Blue Toothbrush* or *Sparky's Magic Piano*. Every now and then there was something unusual requested and one week a fan wrote in to ask for a song that helped shape the rock era.

Listening from his childhood home in Surrey was future guitar legend Eric Clapton. 'The first blues I ever heard was on that pro-gramme. It was a song by Sonny Terry and Brownie McGhee, with Sonny Terry howling and playing the harmonica. It blew me away. I was ten or eleven.'

With the advent of Radio 1 in 1967 Leslie Crowther replaced Derek McCulloch and the show was renamed *Junior Choice*. Increasingly pop music took the place of little white bulls, laughing policemen and tubby tubas. Thank goodness it didn't take over any earlier.

the **nature** boy
meets the sepia
sinatra

In 1948 Nat King Cole had a huge hit with *Nature Boy* composed by eden ahbez. (He liked his name spelled in lower case.) Called a premature hippie, ahbez looked like a cross between General Custer and Ginger Baker when he was in Cream. Legend has it ahbez lived underneath the first L of the 'Hollywood' sign on Mount Lee in the Hollywood Hills, living on a diet of nuts and berries.

Born Alexander Aberle in Brooklyn, New York, in 1908 he wrote his song about a 'strange enchanted boy . . . who wandered very far' only to learn that 'the greatest gift . . . was just to love and be loved in return'. One day he hustled Nat Cole's manager into giving the star a manuscript copy of the song. Cole recognized the old Jewish melody but liked the words and decided to record it. After it was a hit the publishers of the original song, *Schwieg Mein Hertz*, settled with ahbez for a share of the royalties. ahbez had already given away a share in the song to Cole's valet (who subsequently sold his share) for helping him get to the singer, and a further 12½ per cent share went to another man who'd supported him.

Cole recorded another of ahbez's songs, called *Land of Love*, and in the 1960s ahbez even made a couple of records himself. He died in March 1995 in Los Angeles after being hit by a car.

frampton
comes **of age**

Rolling Stone Bill Wyman produced Peter Frampton's first ever single, when the fifteen-year-old was singing and playing guitar with South London group The Preachers. The single, *Hole In My Soul*, was released in August 1965, when the young Frampton admitted that his ambition was to be a session guitarist and listed his favourite musicians as Kenny Burrell, Mose Allison and Solomon Burke.

oh heady
days

The days of package tours threw together some wonderfully strange bedfellows (metaphorically speaking).

Spring 1967 at the Finsbury Park Astoria. The main London show of the tour. Both the Quotations and the Californians opened before Jimi Hendrix. Engelbert Humperdinck closed the first half. (He sang *In The Midnight Hour* and *Release Me*, which was at No.2 on the charts.) Cat Stevens and the Walker Brothers took up the second half.

By the spring of 1967 Jimi was already regularly setting fire to his guitar to finish his performance. Unfortunately on this night he had to be doused with a fire extinguisher, which soaked 'his beautifully coloured stage gear'.

— SOUNDBITE —
'Take a small Bible with you, and read it!'
Producer NORMAN PETTY's instruction to the CRICKETS,
including BUDDY HOLLY, on their first tour away from Texas

pseud's
corner

Former Pink Floyd manager Peter Jenner on Syd Barrett: 'Syd was well into his "orbiting" phase by then. He was travelling very fast in his own private sphere. . . . Syd's madness was not caused by any linear progression of events, but more a circular haze of situations that meshed together on top of themselves and Syd.' *NME* writer Nick Kent on Syd Barrett: 'By this time Barrett's creative processes refused to knit properly and so the results were often jagged and unapproachable. Basically they were essays in distance . . . the Madcap waving whimsically out from the haze. Or maybe he was drowning?'

61

I don't think **so**

Compilation CDs have become the mainstay of a record industry desperate to find new ways of selling us the same old stuff. Albums of love songs have long been one of the sector's staples, along with other themed collections intended to appeal to specific age groups. In the summer of 2004 someone had the bright idea of doing a 3CD boxed set called *Almost There*. It brought together records that stalled at No.2 in the UK singles chart. The oddest mix of tracks is bound together by this tenuous link, so odd you can't imagine anyone actually listening to the whole lot. From the Stranglers' *Golden Brown* you run into Sweet's *Ballroom Blitz*. The Whispers' *And The Beat Goes On* segues into Deep Purple's *Black Night* before CD3 ends with Terrorvision's *Tequila*. Worst of all, though, is Freddie and the Dreamers' appalling *I'm Telling You Now* before Peobo Bryson & Roberta Flack's *Tonight I Celebrate My Love*. It's difficult to see who this album is aimed at. In truth it has no real reason to exist.

the **ballad** of the **hard** rock **kid**

If you think hard rock was a term coined in the late '60s and early '70s then think again. Back in 1949, in Alabama, Hardrock Gunter and his Pebbles were a sensation. Their record *Birmingham Bounce* came out in 1950 on Bama Records and has been cited by some as the track most entitled to be called 'the first rock and roll record'. The song features the word 'rockin' frequently. Gunter's follow up was *Gonna Dance All Night* in which he drawls 'We're gonna rock 'n' roll'. The 25-year-old who was born Sidney Gunter got his nickname from working with pickaxes in the mines around Birmingham, Alabama. He and all the others doing this back-breaking work were called 'hardrocks'. As well as working the mines he played talent shows as 'Goofy Sid', so he was probably pleased with his new handle.

the
sun and
the moon

Ever wondered which album you would come closest to hearing in its entirety if you were stuck on the famous BBC-owned Desert Island? It's Pink Floyd's *Dark Side of The Moon*. Jeremy Clarkson took *Time*, Zandra Rhodes *Us and Them*, Alan Ayckbourn *Eclipse*, and Pamela Stephenson *Brain Damage*. Apparently while she was recording the programme Pamela said this was the song that most reminded her of an LSD trip, a remark that failed to survive the final edit. It's been claimed that the Floyd album has, over the years, been the most popular music in Amsterdam's many live sex shows, which clearly had no influence over the people who picked it. Pink Floyd's Dave Gilmour, when he was a guest on the show, picked none of his own band's records (unlike some other musicians) but chose records that included Tom Waits, Dylan, the Kinks and Neil Young. Dave's choice, if he was only allowed one record, was Martha and the Vandellas' *Dancing in the Street*, which probably surprised many people. For good measure George Clooney took *Another Brick in the Wall*.

big
down under

Australia's biggest-selling album ever was *Whispering Jack* by John Farnham. The excellent fanzine *Zabadak* called him Australia's Cliff Richard and it wasn't wrong. He had his first hit in 1967 with *Sadie, The Cleaning Lady,* but it wasn't until the early '80s that he was really heard outside Australia when he replaced Glenn Shorrock in the Little River Band. It was a short-lived relationship and in 1985 Farnham was back solo. He recorded *You're The Voice,* which became his only UK hit, making No.6 in 1987. It topped the Aussie charts and helped *Whispering Jack* to sell over a million copies.

the twelve british
Beatles albums
– & how many Lennon & McCartney songs they featured

PLEASE, PLEASE ME • 8 out of 14 tracks

WITH THE BEATLES • 7 out of 14 tracks (1 George Harrison)

A HARD DAY'S NIGHT • all 13 tracks

BEATLES FOR SALE • 8 out of 14 tracks

HELP! • 10 out of 14 tracks (2 George Harrison)

RUBBER SOUL • 12 out of 14 tracks (2 George Harrison)

REVOLVER • 11 out of 14 tracks (3 George Harrison)

SGT PEPPER'S LONELY HEARTS CLUB BAND • 12 out of 13 tracks (1 George Harrison)

THE BEATLES • 25 out of 30 tracks (4 George Harrison and 1 Ringo Starr)

YELLOW SUBMARINE • 5 out of 13 tracks (2 George Harrison and 6 George Martin)

ABBEY ROAD • 14 out of 17 tracks (2 George Harrison and 1 Ringo Starr)

LET IT BE • 8 out of 12 tracks (2 George Harrison and 1 Harrison/Lennon/McCartney/Starr)

the twenty-one
Beatles songs
NOT composed by any of the Beatles (in chronological order)

ANNA (GO TO HIM) • Alexander

CHAINS • Goffin/King – a hit for the Cookies in 1962 by the prolific husband and wife team who worked out of the Brill Building

BOYS • Dixon/Farrell

BABY IT'S YOU • Bacharach/David/Williams

A TASTE OF HONEY • Marlow/Scott

TWIST AND SHOUT • Medley/Russell

TILL THERE WAS YOU • Willson – performed by the Beatles at the Royal Variety Show in 1963, it came from the Broadway show *The Music Man*

PLEASE MR POSTMAN • Bateman/Dobbins/Garrett/Gorman/Holland – the first No.1 for the Tamla label

ROLL OVER BEETHOVEN • Berry – The Beatles, the Stones and the Beach Boys all covered Chuck Berry's songs, which earned Ol' Flat Top a tidy sum

YOU'VE REALLY GOT A HOLD ON ME • Robinson – this had just been a big hit in America for Smokey Robinson's group the Miracles

DEVIL IN HER HEART • Drapkin

MONEY (THAT'S WHAT I WANT) • Bradford/Gordy – Berry Gordy was the founder of Tamla Motown Records

ROCK & ROLL MUSIC • Berry

MR MOONLIGHT • Johnson

KANSAS CITY/HEY-HEY-HEY-HEY! [medley] • Lieber/Penniman/Stoller

WORDS OF LOVE • Holly

HONEY DON'T • Perkins
EVERYBODY'S TRYING TO BE MY BABY • Perkins – George sings lead vocal
on one of his hero's records
ACT NATURALLY • Morrison/Russell
DIZZY MISS LIZZY • Williams – Larry Williams wrote it and had a minor hit in
1958
MAGGIE MAE • Traditional

yesterday
once more

The number of covers of Beatles songs has reached astonishing proportions. *Yesterday* alone has over 1,000 cover versions and is the most covered song in history.

Beatles covers include the great, the obscure and the downright dreadful. There are songs like *A Day In The Life*. You wonder why anyone would cover this particular track, but Shirley Bassey gave it her best shot. If it's a laugh you want, try Jimmy Tarbuck's version of *All My Loving* or Peter Sellers' take on *A Hard Day's Night*. For the truly excruciating there's William Shatner's *Lucy in The Sky With Diamonds* on his *Transformed Man* album. For wimpy, check out Plastic Penny's attempt to improve on *Strawberry Fields Forever*.

Many Beatles songs have been snapped up by the muzak makers, like the Soulful Strings' mellow version of *The Inner Light*, *Yellow Submarine* by Enoch Light and His Light Brigade or *Eleanor Rigby* by the Mystic Moods Orchestra. To prove they probably travel better than they arrive there's Marta Kubisova's *Hey Jude* with Czech lyrics or Renato & His Blue Caps and *Love Me Do*. Worst is always subjective, but Frankie Howerd's *Mean Mr Mustard* or Pinky & Perky's *All My Loving* vie for the honour. But then again they may be so bad they're good!

— ONE-LINER —
**It was Paul McCartney's uncle Jack who pointed him
in the direction of music. Jack advised his nephew
to take up the piano, because that way
he'd always be invited to parties.**

65

barking mad

Long before starring in the Goodies and having hit records, the now-famous ornithologist Bill Oddie wrote material and songs for David Frost's TV show. One of the most noteworthy was *Camberley Kate*, which aired in the summer of 1964 and was inspired by recent newspaper publicity about 'the amorous wives of Camberley'. Oddie, quite unaware that there was already a famous 'Camberley Kate', an old lady who pushed a pram around the town accompanied by dozens of dogs, almost found himself on the end of writ. She consulted a solicitor and was keen to pursue Oddie for his alleged public humiliation of her sexual exploits, but she was advised, against her better judgement, to let sleeping dogs lie.

— ONE-LINER —

**Chart-topping Ricky Valance also notched up a
sporting No.1 when he became the
javelin-throwing champion of RAF's Malta Command.**

it's
in **the genes**

Chart-topping singer John Leyton's father owned several music halls, including the Shoreditch Empire and the Cambridge Music Hall, while his mother, under the pseudonym Babs Walters, played many leading roles on the London stage. They wanted him to join the family rope business, but he enrolled at an actors' workshop instead and eventually landed major roles in *Biggles*, *Von Ryan's Express* and *The Great Escape*. He also had a string of hits in the early '60s, including *Johnny, Remember Me* and *Wild Wind* and *Son, This Is She*. On 24 July 1961 the single *Johnny, Remember Me* got the biggest plug of any record to date in Britain, when he was featured peforming it as Johnny St Cyr in *Harpers West One*, a TV series with 25 million viewers.

heartfelt

Tony Bennett is still going strong having made his debut on the *Billboard* charts in 1951. A couple of years ago he played an open-air jazz festival in Glasgow and during his performance of *I've Left My Heart in San Francisco* the large crowd was moved to sing-a-long-a-Tony. Unfortunately as often happens in the open air, with the sound bouncing around, the crowd's timing went somewhat awry and on this occasion they ended up some way ahead of Tony. In a quiet moment a wag in the crowd, with typical Glaswegian insight, shouted out, 'Try and keep up, wee man.'

such a nice boy

On 2 January 1963 an eager young amateur musician wrote to BBC Radio's *Jazz Club*. 'I am writing on behalf of the Rollin' Stones Rhythm and Blues Band. We have noticed recently in the musical press, that you are seeking fresh talent for *Jazz Club*. We have West End residences at the Flamingo Jazz Club on Mondays, and at the Marquee Jazz Club on Thursdays, as well as several other suburban residences. We already have a large following in the London area, and in view of the vast increase of interest of R&B in Britain, an exceptionally good future has been predicted for us by many people. Our front line consists of vocal and harmonica (electric) and 2 guitars, supported by a rhythm section comprising bass, piano and drums. Our musical policy is simply to produce an authentic Chicago R&B sound, using material of such R&B greats as Muddy Waters, Howlin' Wolf, Bo Diddley, Jimmy Reed and many others. We wonder if you can possibly arrange for us an audition. We look forward eagerly to hearing from you. Yours faithfully, Brian Jones.'

PR man's dream

After Frank Sinatra left Tommy Dorsey's band and went solo, he was billed at his first major gig (with Benny Goodman) as 'The Voice That Has Thrilled Millions'. His publicist had a bright idea – he shortened it to The Voice. There have been many similar epithets, but sadly a good moniker isn't always enough. Some of those that follow are so obscure you've probably never heard of them.

ALMA COGAN • The Girl With The Laugh in her Voice.
BRENDA LEE • Little Miss Dynamite
DANNY PURCHES • The Singing Gypsy Boy
DICK DALE • The King of The Surf Guitars
DICKIE PRIDE • The Sheik of Shake
ELLA MAE MORSE • The Queen of Rock'n'Roll
FRANK WEIR • The Pied Piper of The Twentieth Century
FRANKIE LAINE • Mr Rhythm
GENE CHANDLER • The Duke of Earl
GENE PITNEY • The Rockville Rocket
JAMES BROWN • The Godfather of Soul
JANIS MARTIN • The Female Elvis
JOHNNY CASH • The Man In Black
JOHNNY HALLIDAY • The Pope of Rock
JOHNNY RAY • The Cry Guy, The Nabob of Sob, The Prince of Wails, The Atomic Ray
LARRY PAGE • The Singing Rage
MIKE MERCADO • The Swinging Monk.
NANA MOUSKOURI • The Voice of Nostalgia
RIC RICHARDS • A Voice in a Million
ROBERT WILSON • The Voice of Scotland
RUBY MURRAY • The Heartbeat Girl

top tips from the stars

Ever wanted to write a classic pop song? According to Neil Tennant of the Pet Shop Boys it's simple: 'A flat, B flat, G minor 7th, C minor. That's the chord change. A guaranteed world-wide hit.' They're the chords of Rick Astley's *Never Gonna Give You Up* and most of Stock, Aitken & Waterman's biggest hits.

piano **man**

Steely Dan, as everyone knows, are Walter Becker and Donald Fagen. Their eight classic albums from 1972's *Can't Buy A Thrill* to 1980's *Gaucho* were all written entirely by Becker and Fagen with the exception of one cover, Duke Ellington's *East St Louis Toodle-oo*, *Gaucho*'s title track, which was co-written with jazz pianist extraordinaire Keith Jarrett; and *The Fez*, written with pianist Paul Griffin. Griffin was also the man who played piano on Dylan's *Like A Rolling Stone* and Don McLean's *American Pie*.

breeding

For the most part session men are a breed apart, but an integral ingredient in the business of hits. Many future stars got their start by adding their talent to other people's recordings for a nominal 'session fee'. Elton John tinkled the ivories for Tom Jones on his 1968 big hit *Delilah*. Reg, as he was known back then, also made a healthy little living working on numerous hits compilations in the late '60s and early '70s. *Chartbusters Risin'* from 1970 includes his version of *Young Gifted and Black*, while *Pick of The Pops Vol.4* has Reg's take on Mungo Jerry's *In The Summertime*.

Jimmy Page, before Led Zeppelin, played on so many hits that it's tricky to list them all; bizarrely, some have credited Jimmy with playing on between 50 and 90 per cent of ALL the singles released over a couple of years in the '60s. That's what happens when you become a legend. Jimmy would be very proud of some, like Joe Cocker's *With A Little Help From My Friends* or the Who's *I Can't Explain*; not so, perhaps, Val Doonican's *Walk Tall*.

The brilliant bass player Herbie Flowers played on Clive Dunn's *Grandad* (and he wrote it!) as well as Lou Reed's *Walk On The Wild Side*. And there's Peter Gabriel's flute on Cat Stevens' *Lady D'Arbanville*, Tim Rice doing B/Vs on Scaffold's *Lily The Pink* and Billy Joel playing piano on the Shangri-La's *Leader of The Pack*. Unfortunately for Billy, he didn't get a session fee because he wasn't a member of the union.

dan **dare**

Back in 1971 Barbra Streisand released an album entitled *Barbra Joan Streisand*, probably because that's her name. Anyway, as well as covering a couple of John Lennon songs and three by Carole King she also did *I Mean To Shine* by Walter Becker and Donald Fagen, soon to be of Steely Dan fame. It was the first of their songs to be recorded by another artist. On the track Fagen plays organ, June Millington (who had been in the all-girl band Fanny) plays guitar and Bobby Keys (long-time Stones sideman) plays sax. Everybody has to start somewhere.

it's not true

'It's extremely easy to listen to the new Spandau Ballet LP and even easier to forget it,' said Steve Lake in the *Melody Maker* review of *True*, which went on to be a No.1 album in the UK in 1983 and spent 90 weeks on the chart. It also produced three top 10 singles, including the chart-topping *True* and *Gold*, which reached No.2. In his damning review Lake didn't even think *True* or *Gold* were worthy of a mention; you might think, of course, that this was perceptive reviewing.

son, you're **no** longer **a bachelor** boy

The Bachelors were one of the most successful groups on the British charts during the 1960s. In fact they spent more weeks on the chart during the decade than any other British band except the Beatles, the Shadows and the Hollies. The Bachelors were John Stokes, and brothers Conleth and Declan Cluskey, who were affectionately known as Con and Dec; John was called John. The trio stayed together until the mid-1980s when rather unexpectedly the brothers Cluskey ousted John, apparently citing the fact that he couldn't sing as the reason for his going. John went on to tour with his own band, the nattily named John Stokes' Bachelors.

Freddie mercury's
balls

In 1976 Freddie Mercury came clean about his own favourite dish, admitting that it was pork balls in tomato sauce. Here's Freddie's personal recipe:

> 1 small onion
> 8oz lean pork
> 1 thick slice from a small loaf
> 1 egg yolk
> Salt and pepper
> Can of condensed cream of tomato soup
> ¼ can of water

Chop the onion finely. Put the meat through a mincer (for a smooth texture). Soak the bread in water then squeeze it out. Add to the pork, onion, egg yolk, salt and pepper. Roll the mixture into large balls about 2 inches in diameter. Mix the tomato soup and water and bring to the boil. Drop the pork balls into this sauce, cover and simmer for 45 minutes.

marc **III**

A firm believer that people are reincarnated, Marc Bolan claimed to have been on earth three times as different characters. On the first occasion he reckoned he was a cavalier. Later he came back as a wandering minstrel, before returning in 1947 as Marc Feld. He also claimed to have gone into old houses that he'd never seen before and known their layout and history. Look out for the comeback then.

—— ONE-LINER ——
Before he was famous Bob Dylan briefly played piano for Bobby Vee. He later masqueraded as his former boss!

fantasy
top of **the pops**

On some No.1 records the label would have read much better if someone else had recorded them. I offer you . . .

TWO LITTLE BOYS • Ant & Dec
99 RED BALLOONS • Puff Daddy
A WHITER SHADE OF PALE • Cream
RETURN TO SENDER • The Singing Postman
NUT ROCKER • Ozzy Osbourne
THE YOUNG ONES • The Rolling Stones
FLYING WITHOUT WINGS • Pilot
BARBIE GIRL • Barbra Streisand
WALKING ON THE MOON • Steps
KNOCKIN' ON HEAVEN'S DOOR • Mercury Rev
TEARS ON MY PILLOW • Tears For Fears
HOLD ME CLOSE • Squeeze
HE AIN'T HEAVY, HE'S MY BROTHER • Karen Carpenter
DOCTORIN' THE TARDIS • The Who
I'M YOUR MAN • Boy George
WEST END GIRLS • East 17
BILLIE JEAN • King
EBONY & IVORY • Mrs Mills
NO CHARGE • Free
LITTLE RED ROOSTER • Chicken Shack
CAN THE CAN • Can
CHIRPY CHIRPY CHEEP CHEEP • The Byrds

on the
subject
of **prats**

Johnny Reggae by the Piglets got to No.3 in 1971 and has been described as 'the biggest and best white reggae song ever written' by Jonathan King. Of course this prattle comes from the man who just happened to be the Piglets.

— ONE-LINER —
The Cascades, who had a big transatlantic hit with
***Rhythm Of The Rain* in 1963, took their name**
from a brand of soap.

radio
slightly gaga

In early 1961 BBC DJ Pete Murray 'took a hefty swipe at Rock 'n' Roll', according to the *Melody Maker*. He was about to start a new show on the BBC's Light Programme and told the paper that he would play no rock. According to Pete, 'I hate Rock 'n' Roll. It must be the only form of music which the majority of musicians who are playing it dislike too. They only do it because it's popular with the kids. I reckon the people who play rock are those who hate it more than anyone else.' Pete, in addition to being the first person ever to say the 'f word' on air during his days as a Radio Luxembourg DJ in 1953, became one of the original Radio 1 DJs in 1967.

spot
the bore

John Peel's *Top Gear* show on BBC Radio 1 regularly featured 'in session' recordings from its earliest days. Just about everyone did these live-in-studio recordings, which included Jimi Hendrix's last ever session. Peel, famous for his monotonous delivery, was not overly impressed with sitting through these recordings. 'I found them extraordinarily boring. I went to a Hendrix one because I realised he was a bit of a hero, but it was still boring.' You said it John . . . boring.

young
gifted
and white

Long before becoming one of the most popular disc jockeys on the BBC, Jimmy Young topped the chart twice (in 1955), had twelve hits, played rugby for both Bath and Wigan, sang in the Three Choirs Festival, was a crack boxer and appeared in the film *Lady Godiva Rides Again*.

pissed **off**
of
penarth

With over a dozen top 10 records and four that topped the singles chart Shakin' Stevens was one of the most successful chart acts of the '80s. His first hit was *Hot Dog* in 1980, but Shakey had been making records for years, plugging away for a variety of labels. In 1970 he cut *Spirit of Woodstock*, which sunk without trace. It wasn't helped when *Disc* reviewed it and gave it a big thumbs down. Shakey was incensed. We know this because he wrote the following week to the paper's letters page, the inspiringly named 'Pop Post', to complain. He said, 'He got it all wrong. . . . What did David Hughes [the reviewer] want? *Summertime Blues* one more time?' Shakey finished off with 'flower power is dead, while rock keeps rolling along'. The letter was signed Shakin' Stevens, Queen's Road, Penarth, Glamorgan.

A few weeks later Ozzy Osbourne wrote from Lodge Road, Aston, Birmingham complaining that *Disc* had confused Black Widow's album *Sacrifice* with Black Sabbath's debut album – which was simply titled *Black Sabbath*. How could they?

— ONE-LINER —
Robert Plant turned down the chance to sing on the original album of Jesus Christ Superstar and the role went to Deep Purple's Ian Gillan.

— ONE-LINER —
Steve Stills auditioned to be one of the Monkees but he was turned down on account of 'his hair and teeth'.

— SOUNDBITE —
**'It's just another one of those,
"just another one of those records".'**
TONY BLACKBURN ON RADIO 1 TALKING DOWN FLEETWOOD MAC'S
MAN OF THE WORLD in April 1969

the
californian dream

The man who masterminded one of history's least competent kid-
nappings, that of Frank Sinatra Jnr, had gone to University High
School in Beverley Hills with Junior's sister Nancy. Barry Keenan
was arrested soon after the botched kidnap in December 1963
and at the time of his arrest the 23-year-old was already a
successful businessman. He had, by his own admission, been
brought low by an addiction to prescription drugs after injuring his
back while avoiding a dog that crossed the road in front of his car.

He had told his friend Dennis Torrence about his kidnapping
plans; Dennis was better known as Dean, one half of surf duo Jan
and Dean. Dean even lent Keenan money while he was planning
the kidnapping and again while he and his two partners were
holding Junior. Jan and Dean had their first hit record in 1958 and
made No.1 in July 1963 with *Surf City*. 'You know we're either out
surfin' or we got a party goin' – Jan Berry and Brian Wilson's lyrics
somehow got lost on Dean. The day that Junior was kidnapped
their latest single, *Drag City* entered the charts; no doubt Junior
found it a little more than a drag.

Keenan wound up spending four and half years in jail and after
his release he became a property developer. By 1983 he was
worth $17 million, although the years since the kidnapping had
been far from plain sailing because in the late '80s he almost died
from alcoholism. But he kicked his habit, opened a number of
treatment centres and made another fortune, occasionally running
across Junior at parties in Hollywood.

Jan and Dean had more hit records until Jan had a near fatal
car accident in 1966. They had a kind of a comeback in the '70s
and '80s playing the revival circuit but Jan was never the same
and died in 2004.

tinkling

Songwriter Barry Mason and his partner Les Reed were delighted with Tom Jones's cover of their song *Delilah*, and were thrilled to see it go into the chart. So it was a happy Barry who stopped on the M1 to relieve himself on the way to see his mother in Lancashire. While he was standing at the urinal, the guy next to him, a lorry driver, was doing what many blokes do while having a wee . . . whistling. To Barry's delight he was whistling *Delilah*, and so he turned proudly towards him with a smile: 'I wrote the lyrics to that song you're whistling.' Back came the reply from the unimpressed lorry driver: 'I ain't whistling the f***in' lyrics.'

— ONE-LINERS —

The King of the twist, Chubby Checker, received his silver disc for 250,000 British sales of *Let's Twist Again* on board the *Queen Elizabeth* while it was docked at Southampton.

The first song that Nat King Cole played on the piano was *Yes, We Have No Bananas*.

he's
a one

Robbie Williams second No.1 record was 1999's *She's The One*, a song written by Karl Wallinger of World Party – a band whose eight singles managed just 29 weeks on the UK singles chart between them. The royalties from Robbie's record must have been colossal as the song also featured on his album *I've Been Expecting You*. Now, you would think that Karl would have been very happy, but shortly after Robbie was atop the charts Mr Wallinger was moved to say, 'I suppose I should have written Robbie Williams a thank you for covering *She's The One*. Then again, I wasn't sure if he could read.'

oh ye of little substance

Over the years the music press has delighted in inviting guest reviewers to pass judgement on new releases. In February 1983 the *Melody Maker* asked Nick Rhodes of Duran Duran to do the honours. *Hungry Like the Wolf*, *Save A Prayer* and *Rio* had all graced the top 10 in the previous year.

Among the singles Rhodes was asked to review was a new one from a band who had released two records that managed to make the top 75 (just) in the past two years. Their new song, *Sweet Dreams (Are Made of This),* was, according to the Duranie keyboard player, of 'little substance . . . It passes without noticing. I've already forgotten how it goes and don't expect to be remembering it in the near future. It lacks excitement and feeling, waiting for the mega hook to no avail.' It was, of course, the record that broke the Eurythmics, making No.2 in the UK and topping the US charts.

do you, ken?

In May 1972 a young reporter on the *South Wales Echo* was given the job of reviewing the new Stones album, *Exile On Main Street*. 'The Rolling Stones have a talent for survival,' he said. 'They've been a monster success for almost a decade. But I've an awful feeling it won't last much longer. With their new double album they seem to have reached a dead end.' His name was Ken Follett and the review was printed six years before his eleventh novel, *The Eye Of The Needle*, became a best-seller.

big sales **from** the **outset**

Getting to the bottom of which artist has sold the most albums worldwide is a very tricky business, not least because record companies are masters of exaggeration and hyperbole. However, you can be fairly certain that the Beatles have sold the most, although country singer Garth Brooks might run them a pretty close second. But then again the runner-up could be Michael Jackson, whose *Thriller* album has sold over 50 million copies. Not far behind are the Eagles; their *Greatest Hits 1971–75* has recorded sales in excess of 40 million. Others who feature in the top 10 all-time album sales list are Pink Floyd, Led Zeppelin, AC/DC, Whitney Houston, Bruce Springsteen and Shania Twain.

hardback **writers**

Shortly before *The Beatles Anthology* book came out in 2000 the press reported that Paul, George, Ringo and Yoko would split profits of £1 billion. Even allowing for some pretty optimistic (and brilliant) salesmen this would have meant, and being generous on the royalties, that they would have had to sell something like 15 million copies. They didn't and the moral is – beware of spin.

don't throw **your love** away

When David Bowie's former manager Leslie Conn went off to live in Majorca, he left some of his stuff in his mother's garage. One day a few years later she asked him what he wanted her to do with the hundreds and hundreds of boxes of Bowie's first ever single, *Liza Jane*, released under the name Davie Jones and the King Bees. He told her to throw them away, which she did. The single now fetches £600 a copy.

as bad
as it
gets

In 1977 DJ Kenny Everett famously compiled and broadcast the All-Time Worst Top 30 as voted for by radio listeners. Over the ensuing years, many have claimed to be in this definitive chart, while others have insisted that they weren't! To settle all arguments, here is that top 30.

1 *I Want My Baby Back* • Jimmy Cross

2 *Wunderbar* • Zara Leander

3 *Paralysed* • The Legendary Stardust Cowboy

4 *The Deal* • Pat Campbell

5 *Transfusion* • Nervous Norvus

6 *This Pullover* • Jess Conrad

7 *Spinning Wheel* • Mel and Dave

8 *Lauri* • Dickie Lee

9 *A Lover's Concerto* • Mrs Miller

10 *I Get So Lonely* • Tania Day

11 *The Drunken Driver* • Ferlin Huskey

12 *Runk Bunk* • Adam Faith

13 *Why Am I Living?* • Jess Conrad

14 *29th September* • Equip 84

15 *Surfin' Bird* • The Trashmen.

16 *Let's Get Together* • Hayley Mills

17 *Mechanical Man* • Bent Bolt and the Nuts

18 *I'm Going To Spain* • Steve Bent

19 *The Big Architect* • Duncan Johnson

20 *Cherry Pie* • Jess Conrad

21 *Dotty* • The Most Brothers

22 *Kinky Boots* • Honor Blackman and Patrick McNee

23 *The Shifting Whispering Sands* • Eamonn Andrews

24 *My Girl* • Floyd Robinson

25 *Revelation* • Daniel

26 *Goin' Out Of My Head* • Rafael

27 *Made You* • Don Duke

28 *My Feet Start Tapping* • Adolf Bagel

29 *Hey Little Girl* • Ray Sharp

30 *The Puppet Song* • Hughie Green

poodle **power**

In 1964 the Rolling Stones were on a 29-date package tour around Britain headlined by John Leyton and including singers Billie Davis, Mike Berry and Mike Sarne. Also on the tour was Jet Harris, who had quit the Shadows a couple of years earlier and more recently broken up with his drummer partner Tony Meehan. According to Bill Wyman, Jet proved to be an interesting character.

'In York [halfway through the tour] I noticed that Jet Harris had a whole crate of light ale in his dressing room. I was told he had one each night, and drank the lot all by himself! I was also amazed when I found out that he didn't play his bass on stage, but that he mimed to it, while Billy Kuy of the Innocents played Jet's parts, hidden behind the curtains. On the last night Jet got drunk and told dirty jokes throughout his set to a stunned audience. As if responding to Jet's performance, Billie Davis's poodle walked onstage, peed on Jet's spot-lit vocal mic stand while he was singing and walked off.' Rock 'n' roll!

a glimmer of **talent**

The first Jagger/Richards song to make the US charts was Gene Pitney's *That Girl Belongs To Yesterday*. It got to No.49 in February 1964. Three months later the Stones had their first *Billboard* hit with *Not Fade Away*, which got one place higher than Pitney's record. *Not Fade Away* was originally a hit for Buddy Holly and the Crickets. The Stones' second US hit, *Tell Me (You're Coming Back To Me)* was their first self-penned recording. It made No.24 in July 1964.

— HEADLINE NEWS —

FRANKIE GOES TO HOLLYWOOD

The headline in *Variety* when Frank Sinatra moved out to California in 1943 to seek his fortune in the movies.

the eyelashes have it

Back in 1983 a young student from University College London teamed up with another final year undergraduate to form a band they called Seona Dancing, who very soon signed to Decca. 'We've never consciously written songs with the chart in mind, thinking this song will get to number so-and-so, but if they do chart that's very pleasing – and it means people have heard your record. If thirteen-year-old girls want to buy the single because of our long eyelashes then great.' Now go back, think of the TV show *The Office*, and reread what the young student had to say in a David Brent-like voice. One half of Seona Dancing was none other than Ricky Gervaise, before he dropped the 'e' to became world famous. His biog listed him as coming from Reading and liking zippy philosopher and libertarian John Stuart Mill.

the Is have it

One thing is certain in the heady world of pop music – believing in yourself moves you a whole lot closer to your goal. Marc Bolan's self-confidence was unshakeable. He knew that he was destined to be a star. 'I just knew I would be famous . . . don't ask me how, I just knew. I used to like Elvis and Cliff when I was a kid and had some idea that my time would come when people would idolize me in the same way. . . . I was right, wasn't I?"

who is it? . . . it's his bobness!

In 1997 Bob Dylan played in front of over 250,000 people, including His Holiness Pope John Paul II. Naturally Dylan performed *Knockin' On Heaven's Door*. Only time will tell how well it went down.

spin

The most unpopular name for male singers seems to be Webb. Harry Webb changed his name to Cliff Richard, Gary Webb changed his name to Gary Numan, while early '60s EMI artist Peter Webb became Mark Tracey. But then it didn't seem to worry Stan Webb or Jimmy Webb.

the voice of reason

Twenty or so years ago Adam Sweeting was reviewing singles at the *Melody Maker*. (He now contributes regularly to the *Guardian*, among other broadsheets.) One week in 1983 he began his full-page review of the week's releases with a statement damning the collective output of the recording industry. 'Hardly any of them should have been released in the first place. Awful records are killing music.'

Running down the list you could see his point. A Julie Andrews and Johnny Cash duet on *Love Me Tender*, Asia, the Style Council, Billy Joel, and Spandau Ballet's *Gold* all came in for a drubbing. He had few good words to say about anything, but did manage the following: 'In a week largely unsullied by decent records this is . . . reasonable.' It was REM's first single, *Radio Free Europe*. It failed to make the UK charts and it would be another four years before *The One I Love* just missed the top 50 (No.51) in 1987. However, they did have some small album success over the intervening years.

— SOUNDBITE —
IS THIS THE SHORTEST ALBUM REVIEW EVER?
'Burn' – Charles Shaar Murray on *Poet, Fool or Burn* by Lee Hazlewood (Nancy Sinatra's svengali).
Succinct and to the point. The only trouble is, the album was actually called Poet, Fool or BUM!

grammys

The first Grammy Awards ceremony organized by the National Academy of Recording Arts and Sciences in America took place on 4 May 1959. It has been said that the Grammys were founded by a group of record company executives who were worried by the advances of rock 'n' roll and, by definition, the attack this new music was mounting on popular traditional artists. It was very obvious from the nominations that the awards were skewed towards the established order. Despite having two No.1 records Elvis didn't even receive a nomination. Similarly, the Everly Brothers, who had had a great year, failed to win anything, although two of their records were nominated in the 'Best Country and Western' category. It was won by the Kingston Trio's *Tom Dooley*, which was even less C&W than the Everlys. The winner of both the 'Best Song' and 'Best Record of the Year' was an Italian, Domenico Modugeno. His *Nel Blu Dipinto Di Blu*, better known as *Volare*, cleaned up, having only managed third place in the Eurovision Song Contest. It was a trend that was to continue. At the ceremony in 1965 the award for 'Best Rock and Roll Recording' went to Petula Clark for *Downtown*. The judges considered it vastly superior to any of the Beatles' four US No.1s.

boy
oh boy

It's a popular myth that every Boyzone single has made the top 5 of the UK singles chart. It's claimed that their first was *Love Me For a Reason* in 1994: in fact their first single was a cover of the Detroit Spinners' *I'm Working My Way Back To You* and despite being a big hit in Ireland it failed to make the UK charts. Nevertheless they had fifteen top 5 records in a row, a feat that may never be beaten.

boyo
boy

Tom Jones had his first No.1 album with *20 Greatest Hits* in the spring of 1975. It was almost a quarter of a century later, in October 1999, that he had his second with *Reload*. It's another one of those records that may never be beaten.

abba gold –
the fantasy
album

Abba's greatest hits album has sold close to 4 million copies in Britain alone, so it's not too surprising that the songs have been covered widely. But they are one of the few bands – beyond the Beatles – to attract so many other artists to cover their work. Here's an alternative *Gold*:

DANCING QUEEN • Richard Clayderman
KNOWING ME, KNOWING YOU • The Wondermints
TAKE A CHANCE ON ME • Sid Vicious
MAMMA MIA • Martine McCutcheon
LAY ALL YOUR LOVE ON ME • Erasure
SUPER TROUPER • Headless Chickens
I HAVE A DREAM • Daniel O'Donnell
THE WINNER TAKES IT ALL • Michael Ball
MONEY, MONEY, MONEY • Eton College Choir
SOS • Peter Cetera
CHIQUITITA • Sinèad O'Connor
FERNANDO • Sex Mob
VOULEZ VOUS • Culture Club
GIMME! GIMME! GIMME! (A MAN AFTER MIDNIGHT) • Leather Nun
DOES YOUR MOTHER KNOW? • The San Francisco Gay Men's Chorus
ONE OF US • Just Friends
THE NAME OF THE GAME • James Last
THANK YOU FOR THE MUSIC • Vera Lynn
WATERLOO • Panpipes

wired for
sound or strapped
for cash?

Thirty years ago the world was a more caring place. In 1974 the members of Dynamite International, a group of people dedicated to the support of Cliff Richard, clubbed together and raised £37 to buy him a birthday present, as they did every year. In 1973 they had managed £30 and bought Cliff a tape recorder. In 1974 Annette Bauer, spokeswoman for Dynamite, said, 'It's difficult to think up ideas every year, so we gave him the money instead. He's just moved into a new home in South London. It's very likely the money will be spent on the house.'

it's **the** taking part

Every book about the charts has lists and comments about the artists with the most No.1s, the one-hit wonders and the like. But spare a thought for those artists who have released a large number of singles and never made the UK top 10. More often than not they are rock bands. Saxon's best performing single, *And The Band Played On*, got to No.12 in 1981. Having already released five singles that failed to crack the 10, they took their own words to heart and had another nine records that barely even troubled the top 30. The Alarm had sixteen records, none of which got higher than No.17. The Mission had one more non-big hit, and their best agonizingly got to No.11. Thunder have had eighteen hits, the best of which got to No.18. The most frustrated of all must be AC/DC who had twenty-eight records that failed to reach the top 10, although they did have seven that made the top 20. But all was not lost for Australia's finest. They had nine UK top 10 albums, including the No.1 *Back In Black* in 1980.

standing in the **shadows**

There are now sixteen different bands who have spent more than five years on the UK singles charts. U2 were the latest to achieve this feat and they join some distinguished company. The majority have been releasing records since the 1960s, which is hardly surprising. On the other hand Oasis only began having hits in 1994 and have so far achieved over six years on the charts. *Whatever* spent fifty weeks on the chart with eight re-entries, *Cigarettes and Alcohol* thirty-five weeks and *Wonderwall* thirty-four. The highest-placed American group are the Four Tops and the second-placed British band are the Beatles. Way out in front of the field are the Shadows, who have spent 770 weeks on the UK singles charts, which is not far short of fifteen years. There is little chance of their ever being caught.

— ONE-LINER —
**In 1961 selling 85,000 copies a week would put you just inside the top 10.
Now you can make it with 5,000 sales a week.**

bulk **purchase**

In May 1996 the Mavericks' album *Music For all Occasions* made a surprise entry into the UK album charts at No.56; by the following week it was gone. No one was more shocked than MCA, the band's label – there had not been a sudden rush of orders for the album, which was almost a year old. Once the dust had settled and the computer logs had been checked, all became clear. A store in Manchester had sold 14,990 copies all on the same day, to the same customer. Shock, horror . . . the spectre of chart-rigging once more reared its ugly head. In truth it was more a case of garbage in, garbage out. A till assistant attempting to give someone a £14.99 refund had hit the wrong button and registered the figure as albums sold.

every home **must** have **one**

Elton John's *Candle In the Wind '97* became the biggest -selling British single ever when it was released after Princess Diana's funeral, selling over 5 million copies. In America it sold over 11 million, but it is the record's achievement in Canada that is unlikely ever to be beaten. It spent three years on the chart and a staggering forty-five weeks at No.1.

— HEADLINE NEWS —
UP THEIR OWN ART HOLE
Review of the Gilbert Lewis & Mills album in the *NME* 1982, and of course they were because we've never heard of them since.

Elton
gone

While Elton John was performing at a gig in the States in the mid-'70s, someone in the audience threw a smoking pipe at him. The pipe hit him in the face causing him to pass out, whereupon he had to be carried from the stage by several bouncers.

specs
appeal

Elton John began to wear spectacles at the age of thirteen, but in his own words, 'only needed them to see the blackboard and for reading. But I started becoming a Buddy Holly fan and began wearing them all the time to be like Holly. As a result, I soon became genuinely short-sighted!' When he found that contact lenses didn't suit him he decided to go with the glasses in a flamboyant manner, owning 200 pairs by 1976, forty of which he took on the road. One pair was fitted with windscreen wipers, another had 'Wow!' across the bridge while a third flashed his name across the top.

I only **have**
eyes for
hue

The reason that David Bowie has different coloured eyes is that he suffers from a condition called aniscoria, meaning that he has unequal pupils. His eyes were normal until a fight over a girl (Carol Goldsmith) with his friend George Underwood at the age of fourteen. Something became dislodged when George punched him, resulting in two operations to try to repair the sphincter muscles in David's left eye. It left the enlarged pupil permanently open, making the eyes look different colours.

not so **hunky** dory

'I think Bowie, like all good legends, should either disappear or die or at least become a recluse, give up and be remembered for what he was good at. I think he's slowly slipped away into tedium and now he's ruined his chances of becoming a good legend.' Singer Marc Almond in 1983 on David Bowie's new single *Let's Dance*, which went on to top the charts in both America and Britain.

the killer **speaks**

Anecdotes about Jerry Lee Lewis are legion, worthy of a whole book. In 1990 Tom Hibbert was dispatched to interview him for *Q* magazine. It turned into a pretty uncomfortable experience. 'I guess you could call me the King of all music,' said the Killer in response to Tom's question as to whether or not he was the King of Rock 'n' Roll. Jerry Lee was soon on a roll, somewhat bizarrely referring to himself in the third person. 'See, Jerry Lee Lewis has had seventy-four No.1 records. Seventy-four No.1 records, back to back, both sides No.1 at the same time in the charts, in a row, two of them in a row, four No.1 records, two been out at once. Ain't nobody ever done that, not even Elvis Presley.' Er, right. But don't be put off, he did make some killer records.

—— ONE-LINER ——
In 1992 Was Not Was made No.4 on the UK charts with their wacky dance record *Shake Your Head*. Kim Basinger and Ozzy Osbourne shared the lead vocals.

the **fleetwood** mac,
chicken **shack,**
john mayall,
can't fail
blues

Mike Vernon was one of the key players in developing the second British blues boom.

'I'd been at Decca as a staff producer for many years and I'd been working with John Mayall and Ten Years After, and when Peter Green joined John Mayall's band, he and I got more friendly. He made a decision to leave John's band to form his own group, and said he wanted to be part of a new label set up that I'd been running independently through a small magazine called Blue Horizon.

'And so I took a demo session that I did with Fleetwood Mac and offered it to Decca. I said, "You know, this would be a great thing to sign. Put it on this new label, Blue Horizon", and they said, "Oh we can't do that. It has to be on Decca. We can't give you your own label." Peter Green was adamant: he didn't want to be part of Decca because Mayall was already on Decca. He didn't want that association, or the competition, so he said "Go shopping."

'So I went to CBS and they said, "Yes, no problem. We'd love to do this." We signed a deal for Fleetwood Mac, then Aynsley Dunbar and subsequently other bands that included Chicken Shack. And of course as soon as Decca found out that I'd made a deal for my own label with CBS, I was called up to the seventh floor. "I'm afraid you can't work for us and have a label with CBS, goodbye!"'

— SOUNDBITES —

'I love *My Ding-A-Ling* because that one weeny song made my wallet so fat and happy.'
CHUCK BERRY

'Santana have a nice lot of cowbells on *Evil Ways* and a nice rhythm feel.'
PENNY VALENTINE in *Disc*, April 1970

'What Dylan did for my head, the Stones did for my dick.'
BOB GELDOF

'People said they were like a band from another planet. I think they were trying to find out which one it was.'
RICK WAKEMAN on his fellow members of YES

'Little did we know that we'd one day be middle-aged men with daughters who have to go to college.'
JERRY SHIRLEY, drummer with HUMBLE PIE

czech's mate checked

Former Czech Prime Minister Vaclav Havel was a man known for his penchant for a bit of rock 'n' roll. He rarely missed the opportunity of catching a gig by visiting bands, including the Rolling Stones, which may be why he was persuaded to appoint Frank Zappa as the Czech Republic's Representative for Trade, Tourism and Culture in 1991.

Unfortunately Frank, who once famously told the audience at a gig at the Royal Albert Hall, 'Everyone in this place is wearing a uniform', was a little too free with his advice to his new boss. He said that it was 'unfortunate that President Havel should have to bear the company of someone as stupid as Quayle, even for a few minutes'. Unfortunately the Quayle in question was Dan, the Vice-President of the United States of America, and when the US government got wind of the remarks they suggested the choice was simple – trade agreements with America or free Zappa records for life. No matter how much you like rock, running a country comes first and Havel relieved Zappa of his portfolio immediately. Yet more proof that pop and politics are far from comfortable bedfellows.

making
your mind
up

'I am not, repeat not, a groupie,' said Frank Zappa protégée Miss Pamela Des Barres in an interview at the height of groupiemania. She went on, 'I am writing a book called *Groupie Capers*. It's really just my diary from eight years old and we are going to make a film from it.' Fast-forward to today and Pamela has a website in which it is announced, 'Pamela is always available for speaking engagements at your club, college or event. Just email her for more details. Better yet – why not fly Pamela to your hometown to hang out with you and your friends for an entire weekend? For $2,500 plus expenses you can have the best-selling author hang out, meet your friends, answer questions, tell stories of her rock-n-roll exploits, etc. And guys – this is a purely Platonic offer.'

glad
to be **bay**

On the subject of adoring fans who wanted more than anything to go out with a Bay City Roller but couldn't get near them, the band's manager Tam Paton explained: 'Girls call me all sorts of queer names because I won't let the lads near them, but I'm only thinking of the Rollers. The fans can't see through this and think I'm being too protective towards them. I tell you, if I let them go out with girls they'd neglect their music.' Hmm.

— HEADLINE NEWS —

JONI MITCHELL IS 90% VIRGIN

(apparently Joni hated this ad campaign strapline for her album)

it's a **fair** cop

Rod Stewart's 1978 transatlantic No.1 *Do Ya Think I'm Sexy* was 'stolen' according to Rod. 'It was only when the song was finished that I realised I'd nicked someone else's song.' Rod had been to Rio de Janeiro and heard people at the carnival singing a song from which he took the musical hook. It was called *Taj Mahal* (a tribute to the American blues singer of that name) and was a big hit in Brazil in 1972 for Jorge Ben. Rod apologized to Jorge and the latter 'earned a few bob' according to Rod. Interestingly, the song is still credited on Rod's *Greatest Hits* album to Stewart/Appice. Carmene Appice was an original member of '60s symphonic-psych rockers Vanilla Fudge and joined Rod's band in the '70s.

ultimate spin

Joseph Hobson Jagger, a distant relative of Michael Philip, was interested in statistics and his work as a spindle-maker gave him the idea that roulette wheels were sure to be biased if they spun on wooden spindles. He went to Monte Carlo, watched a roulette wheel for several days and noticed that four numbers came up more than any others – 17, 18, 27 and 28. He began betting on these numbers and won so much that the casino closed and didn't open the next day, inspiring the famous music hall song *The Man Who Broke the Bank at Monte Carlo*.

far **from** sly

Few people have had a more public marriage than Sly of Family Stone fame. He married Kathy Silva in a televised ceremony on stage at Madison Square Garden in 1974. He then went on to give a live show for 10,000 of his closest friends.

mergers
& shakers

You might not be aware that the Sutherland Brothers & Quiver, who had a modest hit in 1976 with *Arms of Mary*, were originally two bands; they merged and decided to retain their names so as not to confuse their legions of fans. In a world of increasing corporate mergers and takeovers, what would happen if the same thing became rife in the music biz. Would we get . . . ?

Beautiful South Go West
Swing Out Sister Sledge
The The Love Love & Money
Bee Gee Sting
Stray Cats & Black Dog
Badly Drawn Boyzone
Beach Beastie Boys
Snoop Dogg It Bites
Crosby, Stills, Nash, Wilson, Phillips & Young
Stevie Wonder Stuff
Yello, Black & Blue
Marvin Gaye's Gay Dad
Jam & Bread

exotic
tribute

In the world of tribute bands just about anything goes but you would have to say that Dutch band the Herbspectacles are stretching a point. Their jolly Mexicali brass sound is a tribute to Herb Alpert and the Tijuana Brass.

In a rare move, the worlds of tribute bands and exotica combined in 2003 with an album called *Yes We Didn't* by Thelonious Moog, a 'switched on tribute', as they put it, to the Monk.

teaching the
world

Ask anyone what Little Milton, Freddie and the Dreamers, Vanilla Fudge, Otis Redding, the Bee Gees, Lulu and Conway Twitty have in common and they'll probably be hard pressed. In fact they are just a few of the more than 100 artists who have made commercials for Coca-Cola.

sax over
the phone

At the age of twelve, David Bowie's big passion was the saxophone, which he was desperate to learn to play. In a bold move he looked up top saxophone player Ronnie Ross in the local phone book and called him. The young boy was very determined and said, 'Hi, my name is David Jones and I'm twelve years old and I want to play the saxophone. Can you give me lessons?' At first the seasoned musician refused but later relented, won over by the lad's enthusiasm. Fast forward to the early '70s and the now successful rock star, David Bowie: 'Much later on, when I was producing Lou Reed, we decided that we needed a sax solo at the end of *Walk On The Wild Side*, so I got the agent to book Ronnie Ross. Afterwards I said "Thanks Ron, should I come over to your house on Saturday morning?" He said "I don't f***ing believe it. *You're* Ziggy Stardust!"'

but
did you **like it?**

'Listen carefully to this worthless ballad and you will hear the sound of someone choking on their own halo.' From that we can take it that *Melody Maker*'s Lynden Barber was none too keen on Paul McCartney and Stevie Wonder's *Ebony and Ivory*.

there's
a **ghost** in **my house** #1

Belinda Carlisle claims to have seen ghosts in her homes in London, France and America, putting her susceptibility down to being a quarter native American. 'Once in London I saw a misty shape leaning over me as I lay in bed. The room got colder and this thing pinned me down. No matter how hard I tried, I couldn't move, scream or even breathe. I thought, "So this is how it's going to end."' Then as suddenly as it appeared, it disappeared. Her first ghostly experience had been at the age of seventeen at her parents' house. 'I was alone in my parents' home in California, dozing off in a chair, when I felt something . . . a person beside me. Sparks started flying out of my body and I levitated. I was only seventeen then and it was a really terrifying experience. I had to be treated for my nerves for months afterwards.'

there's
a **ghost** in **my house** #2

Sting swears that Roman centurions walked the rooms of his childhood home in Station Road, Newcastle, and after he moved to Highgate in London he had to call in the ghost busters. 'Ever since I moved there, people said things happened. . . . They were lying in bed and people started talking to them and things went missing. I was very sceptical until the night after my daughter Mickey was born. . . . She was disturbed and I went to see her. Her room was full of mobiles and they were going berserk. I thought a window must have been left open, but they were all shut. I was terrified.' Following the ghost hunter's arrival, Sting now feels that whatever was there has gone and he can now sleep peacefully.

there's a **ghost . . .** #3

Feeling that all was not right in his home at Seattle, Dan Grohl of the Foo Fighters and his wife Jennifer held a séance. Jennifer asked if there were any spirits in the house. Something spelled out Y-E-S, and when she asked what had happened it spelled out M-U-R-D-E-R. To the third question, 'Who?', the response was M-Y B-A-B-Y. After making enquiries, Grohl discovered that in the late nineteenth century a native American woman had murdered her child in the house and had secreted the body in a well. It was said that the mother was restlessly wandering the house until her child could be given a proper burial.

there's a ghost . . . #4

Actor Dan Ackroyd is convinced that he's sleeping with the ghost of Mama Cass Elliot of the Mamas & Papas, who once owned his house and died in 1974 aged thirty-three. 'A ghost certainly haunts my house. It once even crawled into bed with me. I rolled over and just nuzzled up to whatever it was and went back to sleep. The ghost also turns on the Stairmaster and moves jewellery across the dresser. I'm sure it's Mama Cass, because you get the feeling that it's a big ghost.'

there's **a** ghost in **our** studio

When former Beatles Paul McCartney, George Harrison and Ringo Starr went into the studio to record their parts for the 1995 single *Free As A Bird*, they were adding material to a vocal by John Lennon, who'd been killed in December 1980. Paul felt that John was with them during the session and was fooling around. 'There was a lot of strange goings on in the studio . . . noises that shouldn't have been there and equipment doing all manner of weird things. There was just this feeling that John was around.'

oh, the flawed praise

Under its 'Potted Pops' banner, the section normally reserved for songs it thought interesting but not necessarily chart worthy, the *NME* reviewed Procol Harum's *Whiter Shade of Pale* on 13 May 1967: 'A gripping blues-tinged ballad, warbled in heartfelt style by the soloist. Outstanding backing highlights some delicious organ work. Hummable, thoroughly impressive.' Two weeks later it entered the chart, selling 87,000 on the Friday after its release; two weeks after that it made No.1 and spent the next six weeks at top of the charts.

you beck

When *Sgt Pepper's Lonely Hearts Club Band* came out on 1 June 1967 it was hailed by almost everyone as a masterpiece. I say almost, because Jeff Beck was none too keen on it at the time. In fact he didn't even bother to listen to it. 'I haven't heard the record and have no intention of doing so. It's not my type of music at all, so I'm not interested.' Wonder if he's heard it yet?

and in the beginning . . .

'Noisy drumming marks the introduction. I wonder who it is making all that flaming row – probably a flaming youth.' So began a review of Flaming Youth's single *Man Woman and Child* in July 1970. Within the month Youth's drummer had quit and beaten fourteen others to join aspiring legends Genesis. The drummer's name? Phil Collins.

hatchet
man

Back in spring of 1983 one of Britain's best-known music journalists Charles Shaar Murray – a man of strong opinions – was working on the *NME*. He once called Eric Clapton an 'old fart' whose records made him 'ashamed to be over thirty'. So it probably didn't worry A&M unduly when Murray was given an album to review by one of their new young artists, a 23-year-old Canadian rock singer and guitarist of whom the record company had high hopes. He'd already released a couple of singles that had flirted with the charts in the USA and UK and his new album, *Cuts Like A Knife*, had just entered the American charts.

Murray's review was a total hatchet job. 'This album is a prime example of American rubbish. From the Petty/ Springsteen school of Enlightened Rockists, he looks like a cross between Petty and Sting and produces a noise akin to Springsteen writing the worst songs of his career, committing suicide and – as a final act of vengeance – willing the demos to Foreigner. The American charts are bursting wide open to a lot of new music, which raises hopes that rock bores like Adams will find their meal tickets expiring within the near future.' From which we can conclude that Charles was not keen on the new Bryan Adams album. In fairness to Murray, *Cuts Like A Knife* didn't chart in Britain, although it made No.8 in America. However, Adams has gone on to have sixteen top 20 singles in Britain (including two No.1s), four chart-toppers in America, and a whole hat-full of hits. I doubt Charles likes him any more today than he did then.

artistic licence

The use of classic cuts in TV ads has long been a matter of great debate – does it debase the currency? Levi jeans were famously once forced to take out ads apologizing to Tom Waits for using one of his songs as performed by Screaming Jay Hawkins.

The use of one track in particular has always attracted more than its fair share of debate: Pink Floyd's *Great Gig in the Sky* from *Dark Side of The Moon* on a Nurofen ad. Truth is, it's not actually the Floyd. It was a version remade by Floyd's Rick Wright, who was the sole writer of the track, and therefore it's his prerogative to 'take the money'.

muzak maestro please

In bass-playing circles Jerry Scheff is considered one of the greats. His credits range from Elvis to Dylan and from the Doors to Elvis Costello. He began playing sessions in the mid-'60s.

'I started doing sessions for producer Gary Paxton. We recorded in his house; the control room was in an upstairs bedroom, and we played downstairs in the living room. There was no "talk back" so we had to communicate through the drum microphones. He had a four-track tape machine so the bass and drums shared a track. As I was setting up, a group of the oddest people I had ever seen came into the room. They were the Association and we cut their first album, which included the hits *Along Comes Mary* and *Cherish*. *Along Comes Mary* was the first hit record I played on. It had a big, fat bass mistake in the middle of it, but they liked the take and because the bass and drums were on the same track, I had to live with the mistake.

'When Los Angeles radio started playing the song all day long, the thrill of hearing myself on the radio was dampened every time that note would come up. Two years later I was in a store where a "muzak" version of *Along Comes Mary* was playing, and wouldn't you know it, the bass player played my exact part, bad note and all.'

Keith Richard on the subject of 'mystique': 'It's energy, it's electricity, it's whisky and a few other things . . . they're just words. If there's good band on a good night, they swing, things happen. Mystique is not going to be mystique if you define it. If it's definable it's not mystique.'

dog day afternoon

When the Walker Brothers split and Scott Walker went solo he had some torrid times, and for about a year he talked constantly of quitting the business. During this period he called some people about joining their bands. 'I asked Alan Price and Georgie Fame, but Georgie didn't phone me back and I couldn't get a bass and my dog was giving me some agro that day so I gave up.'

whisper sweet words, baby

Between 1955 and 1963 Bluesman Jimmy Reed was a regular on the American singles chart, appearing over a dozen times. His influence extended to Bob Dylan who claimed Reed's harmonica playing and his harp holder were an inspiration, and the fledgling Rolling Stones loved Reed's laid-back, relaxed style. At many of his recording sessions Jimmy's wife, Mama Reed, whispered the words, which Jimmy then sang; it was Mama who wrote the lyrics.

— ONE-LINER —

Randy Newman's physician father wrote songs as a hobby, and had one recorded on the b-side of a Bing Crosby record.

the other
frank sinatra

Being named Frank Sinatra could be a blessing back
in the 1940s even if you were not *the* Frank Sinatra.
The timpanist for the Indianapolis Symphony
Orchestra would often get a better room in hotels
when the band were touring in America. Another
Frank Sinatra appeared in court for some minor
traffic offences but was let off lightly because the
judge thought he had already suffered enough. 'You
have been punished by a cruel and merciless fate,'
the judge said.

he dresses
in dresses

One of pop's strangest, and least successful, comebacks was
made by Kevin Rowland in late 1999. He had not released an
album in eleven years and it was even longer since the glory days
of Dexy's Midnight Runners. Rowland's new album was entitled
My Beauty and was totally made up of covers. In between this and
his previous solo album Rowland had gone bankrupt and battled
against drug addiction and the songs on the new CD were all
intensely personal to his own torment. Among them were
Concrete and Clay, *The Long and Winding Road* and *This Guy's In
Love With You*. A letter written by Kevin to Bruce Springsteen
asking to be allowed to change the words to the Boss's *Thunder
Road* had met with an outright rejection; strangely Macca had no
such qualms.

As one reviewer said, 'If only the rest had lived up to the
opening thirty seconds.' Not the ideal recipe for a hit album and it
bombed miserably, despite some great reviews. Part of the
problem may well have been that Kevin appeared on the cover of
his CD in a dress and panties, and had performed live in a similar
outfit at the Reading Festival.

so bad it's
good

In days gone by there was always a fair smattering of singles released on the back of a TV show or a big event. An FA Cup Final appearance was too good an opportunity to miss. (*We've Got The Whole World In Our Hands* by Nottingham Forest FC and Paper Lace is just about as bad as it gets.) Many of these spin-offs are just too awful to contemplate, but some are so bad, they're good – and if they turned up on Radio 2's playlist you'd just have to keep listening, Kevin the Gerbil's *Summer Holiday* to name but one. Then there's Hylda Baker and Arthur Mullard gamely getting to grips with *You're The One That I Want*. Dora Bryan's *All I Want For Christmas is a Beatle* has period charm, but that is more than can be said for *Baa Baa Black Sheep* by the Singing Sheep. (There was no follow up.)

Freddie **Starr** ate
my hampton

Ritchie Blackmore, who found worldwide fame with Deep Purple, started out playing guitar with a band called the Outlaws. They worked with Joe Meek at his studio in London's Holloway Road. Apparently Ritchie was working in the studio one day with Freddie Starr who fronted one of the best bands in Liverpool before he became a comedian. Blackmore said: 'Chas Hodges, of Chas & Dave fame, was sitting there half asleep with his pajamas on underneath his trousers. You could see them sticking out of his trouser legs. Freddie came into the studio and dropped his trousers in the studio as I was playing. He got hold of his thing and tried to put it in my ear as I was doing this solo. Of course, I made a mistake, and in those days Joe Meek didn't have a see-through screen. He would have to come into the room to see what was going on. He came storming in, "What the bloody hell is going on?", saw us and just went "Ooohh".' Luckily this was before Freddie discovered hamsters.

off
beatles

'Harmonica starts and then this strangely monikered group gets at the lyrics. Fairly strained in their approach they indulge in some off beat combinations of the vocal chords.' This was probably the first ever review of the Beatles and their first single *Love Me Do*.

messiah –
an anointed king
who will
establish justice
in the
world

In 1988 the Screaming Blue Messiahs (remember them?) got to No.28 on the UK singles chart with *I Want To Be A Flintstone*. Their 1986 album *Gun Shy* had staggered to No.90 on the album chart for just one week before disappearing forever. The album *Bikini Red*, from which their Flintstone's tribute was taken, came out early in 1988 and received high praise indeed from reviewer Andy Gill. 'It's got hit written all over it. . . . The Screaming Blue Messiahs have all the essential requirements for survival in the modern world. Strap yourself in.' In fact the album failed to chart, they never had another hit single, a follow-up album two years later didn't chart either and the SBMs are among the increasing legion of 'whatever happened to . . . ?' bands. To be fair to Andy Gill, he was one of many critics who thought the SBMs were yet another band, in a long and ever-increasing line, who would 'save rock'.

lick-a-like

In the latter part of 1962 Brian Wilson made a demo of a song he called *Surfin' USA*. Brian's singing and piano playing on the demo are somewhat reminiscent of Chuck Berry's guitar-driven *Sweet Little Sixteen*. In fact the whole song was built around the chords, rhythm and structure of Chuck's song, which was very apparent when the Beach Boys recorded their hit single in January 1963. It was a situation that Chuck's lawyers were quick to capitalize upon and later issues of the song show a writing credit to C. Berry and B. Wilson.

spot the **difference**

Everyone knows of the famous case of George Harrison unconsciously borrowing from the Chiffons' 1963 record *He's So Fine* for his 1970 classic *My Sweet Lord*. Unconscious or not, it didn't stop the judge from finding against George. Oasis got into problems over the similarity between their 1994 song *Shaker-maker* to the New Seekers' *I'd Like To Teach The World To Sing*, a No.1 in 1972. Hank Davis writing in *Goldmine* recently noted the shared characteristics of Don Gibson's 1961 US No.1 *Sea Of Heartbreak* and Bob Dylan's *Don't Think Twice It's Alright*, recorded in 1963.

dead air

Anyone who has ever been involved in radio knows that dead air is the cardinal of all sins – and it's not much fun for the listener either. Which makes you wonder what on earth the Grateful Dead were thinking about when they suggested to Joe Smith, their record company boss, that they should record air. 'We'll go to L.A. on a smoggy day and then we'll go the desert for cleaner air and that's the rhythm track,' suggested Jerry Garcia. 'The union won't allow it,' was the only response that Smith could come up with. Maybe they'd inhaled too much Height Ashbury air.

not
glam rock, **more**
glum **rock**

Pulp were no overnight success. They may well have
had the longest gestation period of any band to top
the album charts. Jarvis Cocker formed the band in
his home town of Sheffield in 1978 as Arabicus Pulp.
They made their first appearance on John Peel's
show in November 1981 but it failed to kick-start
them to stardom. Their first single, *My Lighthouse*,
came out on Red Rhino records in 1983, but it did
nothing. Ten years later Pulp's first chart success
was *Lip Gloss*, which made No.50. In 1995 Pulp's
album *Different Class*, including the wonderful
Common People, topped the album charts,
seventeen years after the band's beginning.

bobness
in waiting

In 1992 a young singer/songwriter issued a single
called *Birds Without Wings* on the Hut Label. By the
end of 1994 he had released a couple more and
two albums. They all failed to trouble the charts. In
December 1994 Johnny Black writing in *Mojo* said,
'He delivers in spades.' He, like many others in the
know, was tipping the singer for bigger things. Even
Joan Baez, who had seen him on TV, said of his
writing, 'the best lyrics since a young Bob Dylan'.
It took another six years before David Gray found
acceptance with the public at large. His album
White Ladder was released in 1998 and finally
topped the UK album charts in August 2001.
His struggle was such that in the summer of 1999
he played Guildford Live and was billed below
the Wurzels on the third-level stage.

major
chemistry

Mention the names Goffin and King to any music fan over a respectable age and you get immediate recognition. Lyricist Gerry Goffin was born in Brooklyn, New York on 11 February 1939, Carole three years later on 9 February 1942. They met at Queens College where Goffin was a chemistry major and Carole was studying education. They married in 1959. He took a job as a chemist and Carole worked as a secretary while they continued to write music together. They were signed by Don Kirschner and Al Nevins to Aldon Music in 1960 and began working in the legendary Brill Building. Their big break came in late 1960 when the Shirelles recorded *Will You Love Me Tomorrow?* It entered the US charts in November of the same year when Carol was just eighteen and got to No.1 on 30 January 1961, the week before her ninteenth birthday. Before the year was out they had another American No.1 with *Take Good Care of My Baby* by Bobby Vee (it was the era of the Bobbies) and the following year Little Eva's *Locomotion* topped the US charts. They went on to write over 100 chart hits together, most of them before Carole was thirty. On Gerry's twenty-fourth birthday the Beatles were in Abbey Road recording the Cookie's top 20 hit *Chains*, which he and Carole had written.

eternally
grateful

The Grateful Dead took their name from ancient folklore. Originating in German folk stories, the tale centres on deceased debtors, who, unable now to pay their bills, lay open to view without being interred, their remains often being desecrated as well. As one debtor lay dead and unburied, a young man came along who took pity on him and paid off his debt. A little later he encountered a stranger who offered to go into business with him on a 50/50 basis. The man agreed, the years passed, the company prospered to an extraordinary degree and the young man married a beautiful princess. One day the stranger whom he had encountered said the day of reckoning had come and now it was time to share everything 50/50. As good as his word, the young man agreed, thus proving his fidelity, at which point the stranger revealed himself as the grateful spirit of the dead man and promptly disappeared.

— SOUNDBITE —
'The Grateful Dead are just the Pretty Things in drag.'
PAUL JONES, August 1967

wrong way

A 25-year-old Filipino man was stabbed to death on 25 June 2003 for singing Frank Sinatra's *My Way* out of tune during a birthday party. Police officer Noel Albis said the victim, Casimiro Lagugad, was asked to sing Sinatra's popular song during the party in Manila. According to officer Albis, 'Witnesses said the suspect, Julio Tugas, 48, one of the guests and a neighbour of the victim, got irked because Lagugad was singing out of tune. . . . Tugas suddenly attacked the victim and stabbed him in the neck.' Guests rushed Mr Lagugad to the hospital, but he died while being treated. Tugas surrendered and was later charged with murder.

alter ego

The (other) Jackson 5: Mick Jackson (late 1970s disco artist), Stonewall Jackson (*Waterloo* a hit in 1959), Joe Jackson, Tony Jackson (the Searchers) & Chad Jackson (1990s dance artist)

The (other) Dubliners: Bono, Bob Geldof, Ronan Keating & Sinèad O'Connor

(Carly) Simon & (Paulo) Garfunkel (Brazilian musician)

The (other) Smiths: Will Smith, Whistling Jack Smith, Patti Smith & Jimmy Smith

The Spice Girls: Angie Pepper (Australian rock singer), Leah Curry (Gospel singer), Ginger Black (of the Honeys), Poppy (rap singer) & Saffron (backing singer)

The (other) Animals: Mad Dog, Fat Cat, Horse, Mandy Lion & Bobby Bear

(Bing) Crosby, (Chris) Stills, (Johnny) Nash & (Will) Young

The (other) Carpenters: Mary Chapin-Carpenter & John Carpenter (bass player)

The (real) Crickets: Michael Vaughan (Gospel singer), Alan Lamb (multi-instrumentalist) & Phil Edmonds (synthesizer player)

The Four Seasons: Donna Summer, Johnny Winter, Colin Spring (folk singer) & Emilie Autumn (experimental ambient artist)

Go West: Nathan East (bass player), Joe South (guitar) & Ian North (guitar)

Haircut 100: Simon Le Bon, Limahl, Mick Hucknall, George Michael & Andrew Ridgeley

make mine a **large** one

Drummers, as we all know, are considered by many other musicians to be 'not one of us'. This may have been behind Alice Cooper's remarks about his own drummer Neal Smith. Alice claimed Neal found out how many drums, cymbals and bits Keith Moon had to hit and simply added one more to his own kit.

nobody's perfect

Peter Noone, the singer formerly known as Herman of the Hermits, was at Abbey Road when he saw a tape with a label on it indicating that the Beatles had written a song for him. Back in those days such things happened: Billy J. Kramer, the Stones, the Fourmost and Cilla Black were just some of those who benefited from John and Paul's largesse. In a frenzy of excitement Peter telephoned his manager to tell him the good news. But a few weeks later there had been no phone call from the Beatles offering Peter the song. It all culminated in crushing disappointment when the Beatles new album *Revolver* came out and among the tracks was *For **No One***.

missing in **action**

On his 1974 *Dark Horse* album George Harrison covered the Everly Brothers' *Bye Bye Love*, a reference to his recent split from his wife Pattie, who had left him for Eric Clapton. The album credits say Eric and Pattie Clapton are on *Bye Bye Love* but according to George they never appeared on the album. He said, 'I had to write the credits in about ten minutes as I was going on tour and I put "*Bye Bye Love* – Pattie and Eric Clapton". The record company saw that and thought they must have appeared. They typed 'Eric Clapton appears courtesy of RSO Records'. He hadn't appeared on it at all.'

elic crapton

In its review of Cream's first album, *Fresh Cream*, the *NME* was none too sure: 'The Cream . . . really startle the ears with their changes of volume and tempo as they play.' *NME* also appeared to be just a tad confused: 'In Willie Dixon's *Spoonful* you can almost visualize Chinatown at times.'

and
another **thing . . .**

There have been many situations throughout the history of music where it would have been fascinating to have been a fly on the wall. But few occasions match up to when President Nixon had a meeting with Elvis Presley at the White House on 21 December 1970. They chatted about drugs, patriotism and communist brainwashing, among other things

here
starts the
weekend

Ready Steady Go! has achieved iconic status as a TV show that presented the '60s in all their beat boom glory. But like most things from so long ago the memory is sometimes dimmed by the passing of time. *RSG!* did, of course, feature wonderful performances by the Beatles, the Stones, the Animals, the Kinks and just about every great band and singer from the era. But it also had some truly awful moments. Actor Alfie Bass and actress Patricia Burke did a number from the musical *Funny Girl*. Then there was actor Harry Fowler, singer Kenny Lynch and wrestler Mick McManus dressed in Victorian bathing costumes doing a parody of the Newbeats' *Bread and Butter*. Yes, it was as bad as it sounds.

oz
fest

It is said that Sharon Osbourne once shot out the tyres of husband Ozzy's car to stop him from going to the pub – not only because he was inebriated, but also because he hadn't passed his driving test.

play if you feel an attack coming on

Road rage, of course, is not a new phenomenon. It just has a smart name now to make it media friendly. You can probably trace its origins to the introduction of stereo systems in cars, or at least tape decks. The effect of rock in the early days, and hard dance now, on raising a driver's blood pressure and testosterone level seems obvious. But it would be unfair to blame it all on Motorhead or ZZ Top.

It was in the mid '90s that the term 'road rage' seems to have been coined and shortly afterwards Autoglass, the company who replaces windscreens, had the bright idea of running a poll to see which music was most likely to calm a victim of auto frenzy. The winner was good old John Denver with *Take Me Home Country Roads*. Put it in your CD auto-changer and access it in an emergency.

charity work

When the Move's manager, Tony Secunda, decided to use a rather tasteless caricature of the then Prime Minister to promote the band's new single *Flowers In The Rain*, the possible financial downside never entered his mind. A month after its release *Flowers* became the first record to be played on Radio 1 by Tony Blackburn shortly after 7 a.m. on Saturday 30 September 1967. It had reached No.2, kept from the top by Engelbert's *Last Waltz*. Unfortunately Harold Wilson took the offending promotional postcard somewhat to heart and sued Regal Zonophone, the band's label. The judge found in favour of the PM and he decreed that all royalties from the sale of the record were to be paid to charity, a ruling that is still in force. It was all rather unfortunate for the song's writer, Roy Wood, who like the rest of the band was unaware of the management's little scheme. Wood does not receive a penny from sale of *Flowers*.

the
sun

Bobby Hebb's big hit *Sunny* was written the day
after the assassination of President John F. Kennedy
on 22 November 1963. Arriving at his Manhattan
apartment in the early hours, Bobby was so
disturbed by the events of the day that he was
unable to sleep. As he lay watching dawn break the
song started to form in his mind and by the time
daylight came he'd completed what he felt was a
good song. Over the next two years it was turned
down by everybody he took it to, on the grounds
that it had no commercial appeal and would never
be a success. Take heart all songwriters who get
knocked back by record companies without ears –
Sunny went to No.2 in America and made the
top 10 in the UK.

crazy
mother

Arthur Brown, he of the Crazy World, was being lowered on to the
stage at a festival in the '70s wearing elaborate flaming headgear
when his hair caught fire. Fortunately he wasn't badly hurt.

After his musical career went into steady decline Arthur moved
to Austin, Texas, in the '80s, where he continued to make records.
For a while he had a decorating business with former Mothers of
Invention drummer Jimmy Carl Black. There are no reports as to
the quality of their work.

Arthur had something of an ongoing love affair with Texas. Once
after a show in the lone-star state in the '60s, and somewhat the
worse for LSD, he danced naked on the balcony of his hotel,
which overlooked a freeway, while wearing his flaming headgear.
This act caused several startled drivers to run off the road and
Arthur to be arrested.

colour me
orange

When Frank Sinatra (favourite colour, orange) recorded his duets album with singers from across the musical spectrum, including U2's Bono, he never actually met any of them. The whole thing was done in different studios and at different times.

According to David Bowie, when he did his duet of *The Little Drummer Boy* with Bing Crosby for the latter's 1977 TV show it was somewhat similar. 'I was wondering if he was still alive. He was just not there. He looked like a little old orange sitting on a stool, 'cos he'd been made up very heavily.'

The Thin White Duke himself looks a little orange on the cover of his 1973 *Pin-Ups* album. Twiggy shares the cover shot and she was very tanned after a Caribbean holiday. It was decided that she should be made up with a very white face and David, who was looking predictably pale, was given a heavy coating of fake tan to his face.

— ONE-LINER —
**After the Beatles, the British artist with the most
No.1 records in France is Elton John.**

unhappy
dad

As we all know, pop predictions are a tricky business. Many a reviewer, journalist and record company boss has been forced to eat his words. But when it's the artist predicting greatness then the odds of egg on face seem nearly always to shorten.

'In a year's time we'll be on top of a very, very large skyscraper that we'll have built with the amassed royalties from our album.' So said Cliff Jones of the overly hyped Gay Dad in 1999. Said album, *Leisure Noise*, performed pitifully, making No.14 on the charts and managing to hang around for only three weeks. All may not have been lost: a big-selling single could have turned things around but the three that Gay Dad released after Jones's proclamation all managed just a week apiece on the chart.

a **lowdown** **dirty** shame

Singer/songwriter Boz Scaggs was asked to contribute *Lowdown*, a song from his 1976 album *Silk Degrees*, to the soundtrack of a film about disco. He declined as he thought the movie wasn't going to do that well. He opted for it to be used in *Waiting for Mr Goodbar* instead. The film about disco was *Saturday Night Fever*. The soundtrack album stayed at No.1 in the USA for twenty-four weeks, a mere eighteen weeks in Britain, and grossed $50 million in the process.

chicago – surf **city?**

You really do have to wonder how some albums get made, let alone released. By 1964 Bo Diddley's best chart days were behind him. But he was still recording for Chess Records subsidiary Checker and in 1961 Checker got Bo to cut an album called *Bo Diddley is a Gunslinger*, which was clearly stretching a point. In 1964 they released *Surfin' With Bo Diddley*, which is about as bizarre as it gets.

the **american,** **the** german **and** **the** turk

The biggest hit in America in 1959 was by 23-year-old Bobby Darin, an individual who some consider to be one of the great nearly men. His recording of *Mack the Knife* spent twenty-six weeks on the chart, nine of them at No.1. The song came from Kurt Weill's *Threepenny Opera* and was hardly the stuff of rock 'n' roll. It was also the first chart-topper to carry the name of Ahmet Ertegun as producer.

let
the rivers
run

Tony Rivers is a name that is held in great respect by many music fans. His vocal arranging talents are legendary, especially when it comes to putting down some difficult five-part harmonies. Besides leading his own band, the Castaways, and later fronting Harmony Grass, Tony sang backing vocals for Cliff Richard for many years. In the early 1970s he was one of the mainstays of that merry band of brothers who knocked out cover versions for the *Top of The Pops* album series. His first outing was doing backing vocals on Chicory Tip's *Son of My Father* along with Stu Culver, John Perry and Ken Gold. Not long after that they did Queen's *Bohemian Rhapsody*. It had reportedly taken Freddie and the boys almost a month to perfect the original, resulting in close to 200 vocal overdubs, but Tony and the others did their recording in just one night. It was so good that Kenny Everett spliced their version together with Queen's rendition and defied listeners to tell the difference.

kinky
kapers

As dedicated followers of the Kinks will be aware, there has often been bad blood between the brothers-in-band, Ray and Dave Davies. They famously co-wrote a song called *Hatred*, which included the line, 'Hatred is the only thing that keeps us together', and Ray once riled his younger brother on stage with the introduction 'Let's let the little twerp express himself as best he can.' Dave was so angry that he stormed off and played the rest of the set out of vision, from behind the curtain.

— ONE-LINER —

In 1977 the award for the first ever platinum cassette went to Peter Frampton for *Frampton Comes Alive*.

body talk

Interviewing rock stars, pop legends or those who think they may fall in either of those two categories can be a daunting prospect. It's important to remember that they don't really want to be interviewed; they're just doing it because they have a new album/tour/greatest hits package/DVD coming out (delete as applicable). Their opening line often sets the tone for the whole thing and Cameron Crowe's interview with David Bowie in the '70s takes some beating: 'I think I just saw a body drop right outside the window. Did you see a body drop? Let's go outside and see. I know I saw a body drop,' said Bowie.

who's mad?

When put on the spot to choose their favourite record people invariably come up with something bizarre, but few, if indeed anyone, would identify with Liza Minelli. When asked by *Mojo* to name her 'favourite Saturday night record', she was adamant. 'Something hot. . . . *Mad Dogs and Englishmen* by Joe Cocker.'

working **with** dino

According to Joe Smith, who worked at Warner/Reprise Records from 1963, 'Dean Martin was red-hot. However, he hated to learn songs! We had to set him up with new songs on an 8-track in his car, so he could hear them. We would keep trying to get him into the studio, then he'd call out of the blue and say, "Hey, we should record some new records." We'd ask when he'd like to do it, and he'd come back with "How about 5 p.m. today." We rush around trying to get studios and orchestra players. I remember that on one occasion I bought out the Beach Boys' studio time!'

are three chords **better** than **one?**

The late Ian Stewart, often referred to as the sixth Rolling Stone, used to like to shock backstage guests. He would walk into the room where the band were assembled prior to going on stage, and announce in front of their adoring rich and famous guests, 'Come on my little shower of shits. You three-chord wonders, you're on.' The Stones always took it for the joke it was, but there are many acts who had hits with songs that were just one chord. *Heartbreaker* by Led Zeppelin, Smokey Robinson's *Going to a Go Go*, *We Will Rock You* by Queen, Stevie Wonder's *Superstition* and George Michael's *Faith* are just a few of the dozens of one-chord wonders.

nice loons, man

Back in the '70s, when prog rock ruled, Bill Bruford of Yes offered would-be drummers advice on how to pass the audition. 'No known owner of a multi-coloured kit has ever got the job. The only answer is black. If they're not black get out the pot and paint them. Hair should be long but not as long as the lead guitarist's. Suits conjure up jazz bars so a fairly tasteless line in velveteen trousers should do it. Your musical credentials will be scrutinised with the inevitable, "Who did you play with before, man?" Your local clarinet teacher is not a wise response. Name any well-known rock band and by the time the organist works out whether you did or did not you'll be in the band.'

he was **a** thin **boy**

Alexis Korner was the doyen of the early '60s blues scene in London along with his partner Cyril Davies. They started the Ealing Blues Club and their band was an inspiration to many. According to Alexis, 'A thin boy from Ripley named Eric Clapton came up to me at the Marquee Jazz Club and talked about guitar strings. He also used to come down to the Ealing Jazz Club and sing rock and roll songs, like *Roll over Beethoven*. He would simply stand there looking at his shoes, because he hadn't got used to looking at people he was singing to. He was learning guitar, but he couldn't play then.'

in search **of** the lost **chord**

Over the years there have been some terrible records, records so pointless that no one can find out why they were made. And among the terrible have to be counted any album with a title like *The Symphonic Music of . . .*, *A Symphonic Tribute to . . .*, or *The Symphonic (fill in the name of any band)* – basically any record that has symphonic in the title and implies it has anything to do with rock. As soon as any new music fad or craze comes along it spawns a whole heap of bandwagon discs. Disco was perhaps one of the worst: anybody hoping to get a few extra sales added the word to their album. *Disco Round The Moon*, a compilation that included Duffy Power, illustrates the point. Inevitably each new fad allows someone to trawl through the Lennon & McCartney songbook and come up with treats like Café Crème's *Beatles Disco Megamix*. Mind you most people struggled with punk. There was no *Ronnie Aldrich and His Two Pianos Play the Punk Song Book* or *The 101 Strings Go Punk*.

the man **behind** **the** woman

Robert John Lange is hardly a household name, and even if you use his nickname, Mutt, you will still draw a blank with nine average music fans out of ten. He was born in what was Southern Rhodesia (now Zimbabwe) to a South African father and German mother, and went to school in South Africa before moving to London in 1970 aged twenty-two. His first production credit was for Graham Parker and The Rumour in 1976 and since then he has gone on to define the production style known as 'Stadium Rock'. His credits include AC/DC, Bryan Adams (he also co-wrote the monster hit *Everything I Do, I Do It for You*), Def Lepperd, Foreigner and the Boomtown Rats. At the same time he has worked with the Backstreet Boys, Celine Dion, Michael Bolton and Billy Ocean. In 1993 he fell in love with Shania Twain, shortly after the release of her first album. They married and Mutt began working on her follow up album, *The Woman In Me*, which sold 10 million copies. Since then Shania has become the most successful country artist, although these days the clear blue water between country, rock and pop sometimes gets a little murky. The reason that you may be unaware of Mutt's career is that he rarely gives an interview, but he is arguably the most successful producer of the last quarter century.

cerebral **vision**

One man who clearly had his own vision of the perfect record review was the *NME*'s Richard Cook. Tasked to pass judgement on ZZ Top's *Gimme All Your Lovin'* in 1983 he was on inspired form: 'Enough beef in this brazenly sour celebration of a Texas egomania to forewarn of a second rising of the Confederacy, even if the cortex is wired to a supremely lurid crotch fetish. Discipline!'

wasteland

In the summer of 1964 Simon and Garfunkel recorded the album *Wednesday Morning 3 AM*, which came out in October and flopped. Paul temporarily decamped to London in 1965 and cut an album at Levy's Studio in Bond Street in May. It took a little over an hour to make and cost just £150 in studio time. It includes the original solo version of *The Sound of Silence*, *April Come She Will* and *I Am A Rock*. Like its predecessor, *The Paul Simon Songbook* sunk without trace. His publisher at the time commented, 'He's a nice boy, but these songs are much too intellectual and uncommercial.'

fantasy
album

The most successful chart album in Britain for any band or solo artist is Simon & Garfunkel's *Bridge Over Troubled Water*.
It topped the album charts for 41 weeks and stayed on the chart for 278 consecutive weeks between 1970 and 1975. Since then it has spent an additional 25 weeks on the charts, which all helps to explain why it has sold 2.5 million copies in Britain alone.
And other artists have embraced the songs too.
Here are some of them.

BRIDGE OVER TROUBLED WATER • Johnny Cash
EL CONDOR PASA • Placido Domingo
CECILIA • The King's Singers
KEEP THE CUSTOMER SATISFIED • Robson & Jerome
SO LONG FRANK LLOYD WRIGHT • Sal Viviano
THE BOXER • Bob Dylan
BABY DRIVER • New York Voices
ONLY LIVING BOY IN NEW YORK • Everything But The Girl
WHY DON'T YOU WRITE ME • Olivia Newton-John
BYE BYE LOVE • Trini Lopez
SONG FOR THE ASKING • Lori Lieberman

all the young frauds?

Before they found huge success Queen toured with Mott The Hoople and were apparently amazed to see one of Mott's roadies, hidden from the audience by the side of the stage, singing the high chorus to *All the Young Dudes*. None of the band could quite master it.

big sister?

Post-rationalization is one of the prime movers when rock stars come to re-write their own history. Peter Tork of the Monkees took it to a new level when he suggested that Janis Joplin 'loved us and wanted to be in the show. I tried to introduce her into the show. She was game.' She was probably confused, thinking they sang *Last Train to Clarksdale* and were really a blues band.

the food of love

If music is the food of love then these artists are a square meal. The Soup Dragons – Bread – Hot Butter – Meat Loaf – Jasper Carrot – Prefab Sprout – Brown Sauce – Sweet – Coffee – Springwater.

just desserts?

The Sweet have had more No.1s in Germany than any other British band except the Beatles. Their eight chart-toppers spent thirty-six weeks in the No. 1 slot on the German charts, only four weeks fewer than the Beatles' twelve No.1s.

the hillbilly cat
meets the
sentimental gentleman
of swing

Elvis Presley did not make his American TV debut on the Ed Sullivan show as is often said but on CBS's *Stage Show*, hosted by Tommy and Jimmy Dorsey. The previous day, Friday 27 January 1956, his new single, *Heartbreak Hotel*, had been released, but for whatever reason Elvis didn't perform it. He chose instead to do Big Joe Turner's *Shake, Rattle and Roll*. Elvis was on the Dorseys' show again the following week but it wasn't until his third appearance, in mid-February, that he performed *Heartbreak Hotel*.

Elvis's performance on the show certainly didn't propel the song up the charts. In fact it was something of a disaster. The Dorsey orchestra provided The Lip with a stilted accompaniment; cynics have even muttered sabotage.

Tommy Dorsey didn't live to see what he'd unleashed upon the world; he died less than a year later.

pop-**tastic**

At Christmas time 1967 the ITV network announced the launch of its brand new pop TV show, *New Release*, to be hosted by Tony Blackburn. The producers at ITV had their collective fingers on the pulse of pop by getting Anita Harris to write a specially commissioned instrumental theme for the show called *The Margarine Flavoured Pineapple Chunk* – clearly very much of its time. They also filmed a 'zany opening film sequence' featuring Tone and Anita along with the Who, Jimi Hendrix, Arthur Brown and Cat Stevens. The mind boggles, and will continue to do so because none of this appears to have survived and it certainly drifted from the airwaves almost without being noticed.

music
industry
dictionary

angel dust, *n*. a street name for the drug PCP, but also a term oft used by musicians to describe what they would like the producer to sprinkle on the track to turn it into a great big hit. And in some cases to merely make it passable.

big in Japan, *adj*. not big anywhere

classic album, *n*. one that you already have but the marketing bods want you to buy it again in the new industry-standard format

critical success, *n*. no one actually bought the record

cult classics, *n*. few people either heard it or bought it when it was first released but the new SACD version, it's hoped, will have them queueing round the block

eponymous, *adj*. lacking in wit and imagination when it comes to naming a record. (Is it only the music press that uses this word? Has anyone ever seen it used elsewhere?)

mercurial, *adj*. describes an artist who is sometimes good, sometimes crap and almost certainly difficult

minor hit, *n*. no one but a rabid fan can recall its title, let alone hum it

musical differences, *n*. we hate each other's guts, and music

near legendary, *adj*. old and trying to make a comeback

new age, *adj*. when added to the word music it normally means a dearth of melody and a surfeit of tinkly bits

semi-legendary, *adj*. hardly heard of

stage presence, *n*. the playing is only just acceptable, but it's great to watch

asset
management

At the height of their fame Wham! channelled their money through several companies, one of which was called Nobby's Hobbies Holdings.

equality

When Jimi Hendrix played one of his very first gigs in
Britain it was at ex-boxer Billy Walker's Upper Cut
Club in Forest Gate, East London. Jimi was billed as
'The American Top Soul Singer and Guitarist
Extraordinary'. Rather quaintly, the tickets cost
8 shillings and sixpence for gentlemen and
7 shillings and sixpence for ladies.

and the law won

In Colorado in the last century an enterprising judge
had the bright idea of forcing people who broke city
noise limit laws to listen to music they absolutely
hated. Top of the list was Tony Orlando and Dawn's
Tie a Yellow Ribbon Round The Old Oak Tree. In the
UK it would probably be Black Lace's *Agadoo* or
anything by Robson & Jerome.

it's always someone

There's not a week goes by when we don't hear the
internet blamed by the record industry for declining
sales. But blaming new technology is not a twenty-
first-century phenomenon. Back in April 1965 Bill
Townsley, a director of Decca, complained that 'The
pirate radio ships play records most of the time and
this injures our sales.'

— QUESTIONS DEMANDING AN ANSWER #5 —
**Do all ageing rock stars go to the same hairdresser and use
the same shade of brown hair dye?**

radio
ga **ga**

In 2004 on Radio 2 there was a programme about the semi-legendary singer/songwriter Nick Drake called *In Search of Nick Drake*. Somewhat bizarrely Brad Pitt presented it. It's clearly the Beeb's view that the show is likely to attract more listeners if a 'personality jock' is used to speak between tracks. It seems to open up a whole host of possibilities for personality-led shows.

THE CARPENTERS • Harrison Ford (he was one)
ELVIS (PRESLEY) • Elvis (Costello)
LEVEL 42 • Douglas Adams
THE MAMAS & PAPAS • Posh & Becks
SAVAGE GARDEN • Diarmuid Gavin
QUEEN • HRH the Duke of Edinburgh
FRANKIE GOES TO HOLLYWOOD • Nancy Sinatra
MOBY • Dick Dale (King of the Surf Guitars)
OASIS • Colonel Muammar Gaddafi
THE REAL THING • Jordan
DEACON BLUE • The Archbishop of Canterbury
THE BYRDS • Bill Oddie
MEATLOAF • Anthony Worrell Thompson
SIMPLY RED • Arthur Scargill
BARRY WHITE • Cilla Black
BELINDA CARLISLE • Melvyn Bragg
THE CHARLATANS • The Right Honourable (fill in your choice of name) MP
THE CLASH • Alistair Campbell
INSPIRAL CARPETS • Rob Wilton
WIZZARD • J.K. Rowling

jungle rock

In 1955 the *Encyclopaedia Britannica* took a pretty dim view of rock 'n' roll. 'The rowdy element was represented by *Rock Around The Clock*, theme song of the controversial film *The Blackboard Jungle*. The Rock 'n' Roll school in general concentrated on a minimum of melodic line and a maximum of rhythmic noise, deliberately competing with the artistic ideals of the jungle itself.' Nothing much has changed then!

'you don't know what a drag it is to be you'

During the late '70s, there seemed to be a growing trend for young people stopped for motoring offences to give not only a false name, but the name of a famous rock star. The assumption appeared to be that members of the constabulary never listened to pop music, ergo would not recognize the purveyors of such material. If you give a false name to a court of law, things could be made pretty grim, but if you give a false name to a police officer, it's down to him to check it out. Hence in various areas of Britain a 'David Bowie' was reported as being arrested for speeding and a 'Robert Zimmerman' was fined for upsetting the owner of a café. Hard on the heels of these two villains came a report in London's *Evening Standard* that Led Zeppelin singer Robert Plant had been arrested in Atlanta on a charge of drunkenness and carrying a knife. It turned out that the real Robert Plant had been horse-riding in Wales at the time of the offence.

In the summer of 1977 another outrageous chap masquerading as a music icon was caught. The police said that they'd caught a 'youth' spraying 'a word' on a wall in London's Kentish Town. The word was 'Clash' and the youth gave his name as Joe Strummer. It turned out that it was indeed the Clash's Joe Strummer himself and he was due to appear in court in London to answer the graffiti charges. This unfortunately clashed with another gig in Newcastle . . . where he was due to appear to answer charges of stealing pillows and room keys from a hotel. The agent double-booked again!

soundbite

At a £100-a-head banquet in 1977 John Denver spoke to the assembled multitude, 'I personally am taking responsibility for ending hunger in the world.' Right.

hoochie
coochie **man**

For many bluesmen who returned to prominence having originally recorded in the post-war country blues boom, and for those who were discovered in the post-war Chicago blues boom, the pinnacle of their career was the American Folk Blues Festivals in the 1960s. Bass player and composer Willie Dixon was the man who acted as unofficial agent for the German promoters who put these tours together. Willie had a little black book in which he wrote the phone numbers of every player on the Chicago scene. It also had the numbers of their girlfriends so he could always track them down.

When asked to name his favourite gig Willie didn't talk about one of the European shows. His fondest memory was of a nudist camp just outside Colorado Springs in 1949. Maybe it was what inspired him to write *You Can't Judge a Book By Its Cover* for Bo Diddley.

— SOUNDBITE —
J.J. Cale's real name is John Cale.
He added the second J because it looked good.

who do you
think
you **are?**

For his nineteenth birthday Jam front man Paul Weller decided that he'd like to meet his hero, Pete Townshend of the Who. Accompanied by fellow Jam members Bruce Foxton and Rick Buckler, and a bevy of photographers and reporters, Weller trekked down to Townshend's domain in Twickenham, only to discover that he wasn't in. Undaunted, the party moved on to the Meher Baba shrine at Richmond, only to discover that P. Townshend Esq. had left there just two hours earlier, bound for the West Country. Drawing the line at hacking down to the heart of Acker Bilk territory, Weller gave up on his birthday treat.

big **strong chords**

According to a fifteen-year-old Michael Jagger in a school essay on how to form a skiffle group it was all very simple: 'Before any group is started up, there should be someone who can sing really well and a couple of guitarists who can play good strong chords.'

smash hits

In 1958 the American Catholic Youth Center's newspaper *Contacts* demanded of all God-fearing Catholics: 'Smash the records you possess which present a pagan culture and a pagan concept of life. Check beforehand the records which will be played at a house party or a school record dance. Switch your radio dial when you hear a suggestive song.'

basement jack

According to bass player Jack Bruce, reminiscing recently about the early days of the British beat boom, 'R&B was just a new sound that people liked because it was raunchy and very danceable, and very earthy, real and authentic. The most exciting thing when I was growing up was the Shadows, for God's sake! Wow, look at that footwork!'

penny lane **for** your **thoughts**

In 1963 everyone had something to say about Merseybeat. You couldn't pick up a newspaper without reading about the Beatles' antics and every music paper talked of the latest discovery to come out of Liverpool. In its inimitable style the *Daily Worker* had its own slant on things. 'The Mersey sound is the voice of 80,000 crumbling houses and 30,000 people on the dole.'

telephone
codes

In 1963 four teachers at Abingdon School, near Oxford, performed a four-part harmony *a cappella* rendition of part of *The Highway Code* in front of Princess Margaret at the school's fourth centenary celebrations. It was set to the tune of a piece of Anglican chant.

They subsequently made a private recording. It ended up being broadcast on BBC radio, which brought it to the attention of Beatles producer George Martin. He used the group's vocal talents on the b-side of Peter Sellers' spoof of the Beatles' *A Hard Day's Night* in the style of Lawrence Olivier's portrayal of Shakespeare's Richard III – they performed Lennon and McCartney's *Help!*.

The Master Singers, as they were now known, re-recorded *The Highway Code* with George Martin, and it was released on April Fool's Day 1966. It made No.25 on the singles chart. EMI were baffled: 'It's been selling in thousands ever since its release. Why? We haven't a clue. Even if everybody in the Ministry of Transport bought a copy, it still can't account for all the sales.'

During the summer of '66 the Master Singers recorded part of the telephone directory, starting at A. The recording had the group being gradually faded out under an engaged tone and being faded back up at the end of the Zs. Unfortunately their plan to have it released as a single was thwarted: the Post Office owned copyright on the directory and refused the Master Singers permission to quote from it. Undeterred they came up with an alternative in the form of *The Weather Forecast*. Their single sneaked into the chart at No.50 for one week in November '66, after which they went back to their day jobs.

— SOUNDBITE —

**As I was leafing through an August 1967 copy of *Rave*
magazine a news item jumped out at me.
I quote in its entirety:**

'The Jonathan King–Sandie Shaw romance still blossoms.'

dead
men **signing**

Rock memorabilia is big business, and has been for a good while. Like everything in the field of antiques and collectables it's open to fakers and fraudsters – for example, the *Jimi Hendrix Experience Smash Hits* album signed by Jimi, Mitch Mitchell and Noel Redding offered for sale by a leading London auction house in 1995. The only trouble was this particular release came out three years after Jimi died. It was withdrawn shortly before the auction.

With the rise of eBay, opportunities for similar 'mistakes' are increasing rapidly. Recently a signed copy of a *Best of Elvis* 10" album was offered and snapped up for the bargain price of £350. Only trouble was, it was a French reissue dating from the 1980s, close to a decade after the King's death.

divided
by a common
chord

According to Phonographic Performance Ltd the most played record in Britain (on radio, in clubs, jukeboxes and in stores) is Procol Harum's *A Whiter Shade of Pale*. What's most surprising about the rest of the list is that the Beatles can only claim the 9 and 10 spots, and they do it with a rather odd pair of songs – *Hello Goodbye* and *Get Back*. This is even more surprising when you find out that the most played Beatles song on US radio is *Yesterday* and the two songs from the British list fail even to make the top 100. The only song to make the top 10 in Britain and to feature high in the American listings is the Everly Brothers' *All I Have To Do is Dream* (UK No.4/US No.12). Even Rod the Mod's *Maggie May* managed higher than the Beatles. Other UK placings are 2. Queen, *Bohemian Rhapsody*, 3. Wet Wet Wet, *Love is All Around*, 5. Bryan Adams, *Everything I Do, I Do It For You*, 6. Abba, *Dancing Queen*, 7. Elvis Presley, *All Shook Up*.

The most played song on American radio is the Righteous Brothers' *You've Lost That Lovin' Feelin*.

seemed like
such a
good idea . . .

great albums we have barely known and never loved

Adventures in the National Park • Max K. Gilstrap Whistles (1958)

After Hours Middle East • Sonny Lester & His Orchestra (1960s)

Alfred Hitchcock presents Music To Be Murdered By (1960s)

A Touch of Tabasco • Rosemary Clooney & Perez Prado (1960s)

Barbecue from the series 'Music for Gracious Living' • Peter Barclay and His Orchestra (1950s). They did a follow-up called *After The Dance*.

Beatles, Bach & Bacharach Go Bossa • Alan Moorhouse Orchestra (1971)

Bloody Ballads, Classic British and American Murder Ballads • Paul Clayton (1956)

Blues for a Stripper and other exciting sounds composed and conducted by Mundell Lowe (1962)

Caution, Men Swinging • Dennis Farnon & His Orchestra (1960s)

Destination Baghdad • Artie Barsamian & His Orchestra (1960s)

Disco Round the Moon 'CPO's great disco beat takes you out of this world' • Various artists including Duffy Power (1978)

Elvis Has left The Building by his friend J.D. Sumner (1979)

Fastest Balalaika in the West • Sasha Palinoff & his Russian Gypsy Orchestra (1964)

Hap and the Coloured Coat Featuring the Human Host and the Heavy Metal Kids

Herman's Hermits Greatest Hits Played by the Liverpool Strings (1960)

Hot Bagel featuring Hyman Gold 'N' Cello, his Orchestra and Chorus (late 1950s)

How To Keep Your Husband Happy • Debbie Drake (early 1960s)

Introduction to Jazz by the Rev A.L. Kershaw • Various artists (1956)

Jack Diamond Live at the Norbreck Castle Inn, Blackpool (1971)

John Cage meets Sun Ra (1960s) . . . help!

Let Me Touch Him • The Ministers Quartet (1950s)

Little Egypt presents How to Belly Dance for your Husband • Sonny Lester and his Orchestra (1960s)

Mallet Mischief, 'a study in high-fidelity sound' • **Harry Breuer & His Quintet (late 1950s)**

Mountain Fiddler • US Senator Robert Byrd (1950s)

Music For Bachelors • **Henri René & His Orchestra (late 1950s). Cover features Jayne Mansfield**

Music for Big Dame Hunters • Sounds of a Thousand Strings (1960s)

Music For Expectant Fathers • **Fontanna & His Orchestra (1950s)**

Music From A Surplus Store • Jack Fascinato (1960s)

Music To Read James Bond By • **Various artists including Ferrante & Teicher (1960s)** . . . and they did a volume 2!

Music To Strip By (with free g-string) • Bob Freedman & His Orchestra (1960s)

Music, Ecology and You • **Irma Glen (1970)**

Music For Washing And Ironing • The Somerset Strings (1950s)

Perfect Background Music for your Home Movies • **Norman Paris (1964)**

Provocative Percussion • Enoch Light and the Light Brigade (US, 1959)

Satan is Real • **The Louvin Brothers (1960s)**

Shakespeare, Tchaikovsky and Me • Jayne Mansfield (1960s)

Skin Diver Suite and other Selections • **Leo Diamond (1950s)**

Spectacular Accordions • Charles Cammileri (1960s)

Surfers' Pyjama Party (recorded live at UCLA campus) • **The Centurions (1960s)**

Terribly Sophisticated Songs (A Collection of Unpopular Songs for Popular People) • Irving Taylor (1960s)

The Basic Principles of Kreskin's ESP • **Kreskin (1970s)**

The Bearcats Swing in Beatlemania (Recorded in London, England) (1964)

The Ethel Merman Disco Album • **Ethel's album includes her take on Alexander's Ragtime Band (1970s)**

The Plastic Cow Goes Moooooog • Mike Melvoin (1969/70)

The Queen is in The Closet – **on Camp Records (late 1950s). It includes a song called The Weekend of a Hairdresser**

Where There Walks a Logger, There Walks A Man • Buzz Martin (1950s)

the
street of **dreams**

In 1968 Sue Nicholls had a modest hit with a Tony Hatch and Jackie Trent song, *Where Will You Be?* It was the power of TV, and specifically a soap, that did it. Sue, the daughter of MP Sir Harmer Nicholls, appeared in *Crossroads*. She joined the cast of *Coronation Street* in 1979 to play Audrey the wife of Alf Roberts and is still there.

Two people who had very brief relationship with *Corrie* are Davy Jones of the Monkees and Peter Noone of Herman's Hermits, who both appeared in the show as child actors.

chic cola

Ever wondered where the idea for the Chicago logo came from? In fact it was inspired by the Coca-Cola logo. John Berg, the head of the art department at CBS, got designer Nick Fasciano to produce it to his instructions. On the band's first fourteen albums the logo was in the same place and was always the same size. Chicago were arguably the first band to take corporate branding seriously, and some saw it as a weakness.

too **active** to be
the quiet one

Being in a tribute band carries with it the obvious requirement of having to be as much like the band you are impersonating as possible. Some clearly have an unusual view of what their heroes were really like. Kevin Uttley who was 'George' in an Australian Beatles tribute band was fired and took his case to the Aussie equivalent of an industrial tribunal. Kevin's appeal was based on the fact that he wasn't too fat to be George. Unfortunately he lost his case, not on the grounds of obesity but because he leapt about too much to be Harrison.

bogey **men**

Sport and rock music don't usually mix that well, and that's not a dig at Pat Cash and John McEnroe over their minor 1991 hit *Rock 'n' Roll*. But if you had to pick a sport that was the total antithesis of rock music it would probably be golf. There are some who thought that the '4,000 holes in Blackburn Lancashire' referred to in the Beatles' *A Day In The Life* was an obscure reference to golf, but neither John nor Paul, George nor Ringo ever showed any interest in the game – unlike Robbie Krieger of the Doors, Iggy Pop, Alice Cooper and Queens of the Stone Age, who all enjoy a round. Alice (the artist formerly known as Vincent Damon Furnier) Cooper (handicap 7) is not only a very good player, but also hosts his own pro-am tournament.

failed to **score**

In 1994, probably to the annoyance of the majority of the population of England, Manchester United Football Club topped the singles chart with *Come On You Reds*. Here are ten culled from literally hundreds of footie records that failed to hit the back of the net. You don't need to hear most of them to know why.

IN BRIGHTON • Brighton & Hove Albion, 1982
QUEENS PARK RANGERS • The Loftus Roadrunners, 1977
THE BOYS IN GREEN • The Republic of Ireland Squad, 1988
SIDE BY SIDE • Peter Shilton & Ray Clemence, 1980
OH OH OH WHAT A LUV'LY GAME • The Wolves Squad, 1967
HERE WE GO AGAIN • The Hot Shots & The Leeds United Squad, 1991
I'D DO ANYTHING • Rod Hull, Emu & Bristol City, 1974
BLACKPOOL • The Nolan Sisters, 1972
WHY CAN'T WE ALL GET TOGETHER • Crystal Palace FC & Wives, 1972
THIS IS THE SEASON FOR US • Leicester City FC 1974

he's **dwight**

'I wanted to be like Bowie and Jagger. Do I regret it? No. But looking back, did I look a prat? Yes.'
Elton John

banned
on the **run**

The Sex Pistols made it to No.2 with *God Save The Queen* in 1977, despite being banned everywhere. Lambeth MP Marcus Smith said, 'If pop music is going to be used to destroy our established institutions, then it ought to be destroyed first.' The Independent Broadcasting Authority announced, 'Nothing should be broadcast that offends good taste and decency.' *Top of the Pops* admitted, 'It's quite unsuitable for an entertainment show like *Top Of The Pops*.' Radio 1 disc jockey Tony Blackburn said, 'It is disgraceful and makes me ashamed of the pop world, but it is a fad that won't last. We DJs have ignored them and if everyone else did, perhaps they would go away.' Bill Cotton, the Head of Light Entertainment for the BBC, stormed, 'I wouldn't have the Sex Pistols on anything. I don't think anybody wants to see those types of people.' A member of the Greater London Council announced that he would 'use any means within the law to stop the Pistols playing London again'. The ban by Radio Luxembourg, the IBA and the BBC meant that the single was barred from every UK radio station.

never mind
the **rowlocks**

To celebrate the silver jubilee, so they said, the Sex Pistols hired a boat, aptly named the *Queen Elizabeth*, and invited journalists, photographers, associates and early Pistols fans to make merry and hear the band play a seven-song set. No one was too surprised when the vessel was tailed by a police launch, but things began to hot up when the owner of the boat gave indications that he'd taken on more than he'd bargained for. As the Pistols pounded out their songs, the number of patrol boats increased to half a dozen and the *Queen Elizabeth* was escorted into Charing Cross pier. Johnny Rotten and the boys were getting into *No Fun* when the police piled on board and tried to break up the proceedings.

it's a
question of
influence

In the press notes accompanying his cool new album *Reflections In Blue* (1977), the hip, groovy, well-respected blues singer Bobby Bland surprised his legions of fans by admitting, 'I've always admired Tony Bennett, Perry Como and Andy Williams. This is the thing that I based my blues on and I have quite a few of their records that I listen to and learn from.'

one
for **experience**

The first Jimi Hendrix Experience American tour was as a support band on 1967 Monkees' dates. Hendrix quit, complaining that he'd been given 'the graveyard slot', the one immediately before the Monkees came on. He complained of kids drowning out his playing by screaming for the headliners. At the time there was a persistent rumour that Jimi's disappearance was, in fact, down to a complaint from the Daughters of the American Revolution that his act was 'overly erotic'. It probably was, but that isn't why he left.

write **and**
wrong

There are 'songwriters' who have in fact never written a song, Probably the most famous is Elvis Presley. To be fair to Elvis it was Colonel Parker's doing that songs like *Love Me Tender* and *Heartbreak Hotel* have Presley's name on the label along with those of the real writers. Given that the Colonel got somewhere between 25 and 50 per cent of everything that Elvis made, it was yet another nice little earner for the man who was neither a Colonel nor probably born a Parker. If you stretch a point, you can see where the Colonel was coming from. But that can't be said in the case of DJ Alan Freed, whose writing credit on Chuck Berry's *Maybellene* and other songs was nothing more than a bribe to ensure the records got played on the radio.

what's in a name?

The value of a name in music is becoming as powerful as it is in the corporate world. In fact band names are brand names. Probably the best example is Pink Floyd who played to massive crowds in the late '80s and '90s while founder member and writer of many of their best-known songs, Roger Waters, who had left the band, toured by himself. The Floyd played stadiums, Roger played arenas and smaller venues.

Since the '60s the comings and goings in bands have produced some weird and wonderful scenarios. Former Hollie Eric Haydock realized the value of the brand. He tours as Eric Haydock ex Hollie, and he often conveniently gets billed as Eric Haydock's Hollies. He left the band in 1966 after missing some gigs, which meant he wasn't in the line-up for half the band's big hits. His band includes an ex-Mindbender and a former Easybeat. For many years Dave Dee toured without Dozy, Beaky, Mick and Tich – they toured separately. They have recently become DD,D,B,M&T again, but with a different Beaky. There are so many permutations of bands and performers trading off past glories that the whole thing becomes baffling. Among the strangest of all is the case of Classics IV who had a hit in 1968 with *Spooky*. In the '90s there was a band touring as Classics IV that featured none of the original members, but featured Bobby Valli on vocals. Valli is the brother of Four Seasons founder member Frankie and he apparently sings a medley of his brother's songs on stage; kind of Classics IV do the Seasons with Bobby . . . bizarre.

twistin' your tongue in away

Proper enunciation is something that troubles many a DJ. Many live in mortal fear that one day one of country music's leading ladies will release *Dolly Parton's Greatest Hits*.

just
the job

A list of artists who might be favoured by particular groups, organizations or professions.

ROAD RAGE SUFFERERS • That Petrol Emotion
DHSS EMPLOYEES • UB40
LATIN SCHOLARS • Ultravox
ARCHITECTS • Kraftwerk
BARREL MAKERS • Alice Cooper
POETS • Alison Limerick
DETECTIVES • The Thompson Twins
XENOPHOBES • Foreigner
FOREIGN OFFICE DIPLOMATS • China Crisis
GREENKEEPERS • Supergrass
LONDON'S ENVIRONMENTAL HEALTH DEPARTMENT • Boomtown Rats
CAPTAINS OF INDUSTRY • Chairmen of the Board
ICE-CREAM MAKERS • Heatwave
MARXISTS • Scritti Politti
THE RNLI • Lighthouse Family

grounded

In the summer of 1967 *The Last Waltz* was sitting at No.1 for the third week running. Engelbert Humperdinck (the artist formerly known as Gerry Dorsey, who first recorded for Decca in 1959) bought himself a £2,200 Jaguar but told the press, 'I still live in my council flat in Hammersmith and have no intentions of moving.'

give us
a badge

To launch a radio station today takes huge amounts of money, and established stations run on-air competitions giving away thousands of pounds. When the BBC launched Radio 1 all it took was a few car stickers and coloured badges.

very 'eavy, **very** 'umble

Today we all take the term heavy metal for granted, knowing instinctively what it means. However, the origins of the phrase, as it applies to rock bands, are difficult to pin down. Did the rock critic who wrote that Jimi Hendrix's music was like 'heavy metal falling from the sky' in 1967 cause the naming of the genre? Was he thinking of William S. Burroughs's character, Uranium Willy, The Heavy Metal Kid, from the novel *The Soft Machine*. (No prizes for guessing where the Canterbury band of the same name took theirs from.) And, of course, the phrase 'heavy metal thunder' turns up in Steppenwolf's 1968 song *Born to Be Wild*, recorded in late 1967.

waiting on his **bobness**

In early 1966 Bob Dylan was in Nashville to begin work on his new album, which became *Blonde on Blonde*. On the first evening the musicians turned up at the studio around 6 p.m. to begin work. According to Charlie McCoy who played harmonica, 'He came in and said. "You'll all just have to wait. I haven't finished writing the song yet."' They eventually began recording *Sad Eyed Lady of The Lowlands* at about 4 a.m. the next morning.

all **talk**

Talk Talk could somehow only be British, but one of the main influences on their principal writer Mark Hollis was Frank Sinatra. When the band's first single *Mirror Man* came out in 1982 Mark told *Melody Maker* that he had in fact sent Sinatra a number of songs for his consideration. Mark's contention was that there was a lack of songwriting around, with an over-reliance on arrangements. Given where the Talk Talk's sound ended up, with it's pioneering ambient moods, it's hard now to imagine him saying this.

I've had
enough

At the Royal Albert Hall in February 1970, Joni Mitchell announced she was retiring. A year later Frank Sinatra did the same in June 1971 at a show in Los Angeles. David Bowie made his farewells at the Hammersmith Odeon in July 1973. Of course they all came back. Since then many others have retired, and many have come back. But probably no band has had more farewell tours than Status Quo and the Who. Talking of retirement, what about putting together a band with Phil Everly and Tina Turner on vocals, Brian Auger on keyboards, bass player Jet Harris, lead guitar James Burton, and drummer Ginger Baker . . . oh yes, and the Kalin Twins on backing vocals? They all reached 65 years old in 2004.

— HEADLINE NEWS —
THE FILTH & THE FURY
***Daily Mirror*, 2 December 1976, after the Sex Pistols had said that word on ITV's *Today* show with Bill Grundy.**

867-5309/Jenny

San Franciscan band Tommy Tutone, led by singer Tommy Heath, got together in the late '70s and had a minor Hot 100 hit in 1980 before they made the big time with *867-5309/Jenny* in early 1982. Their record got to No.4 on the US charts, but failed to make the transatlantic crossing. Nothing more was heard from Tommy, Jenny or her phone number, apart from the record getting regular spins on oldies radio. That is until early 2004 when someone put 212-867-5309 up for sale on eBay. An opening bid of $250 was called for and after well over 200 bids it had reached a staggering $80,700. The item then mysteriously disappeared from the website.

perfect **harmony**

In an interview, Bruce Johnson once told me about how the Beach Boys were influenced. It's not what you would expect.

'Growing up in LA, white kids weren't listening to white radio. We were listening to KGFJ and during the day – it was an AM station and it was the radio station for the black community – it was 1000 watts. At night, we kind of caught it after school but as it got dark it went down to 250 watts, kind of like the way you'd have to strain to listen to Radio Luxembourg in London or all over England.

'You had Etta James singing *You gotta roll with me Henry* [Bruce sang this to me!], and that was really cool. We, the Beach Boys, listened to rhythm and blues. We listened to *Fannie Mae* on Fire Records by Buster Brown . . . fantastic.

'So down the road here comes the Stones, here comes the Beach Boys. The backside of *Satisfaction* is called *The Under Assistant West Coast Promotion Man*, but it was really the track for *Fannie Mae* – and, for Brian and the band, the inspiration for *Help Me Rhonda* in terms of the track was *Fannie Mae*. You hear the harmonicas going da, da, da, da, da, da [Bruce sang this too]. You'd be surprised at all the kind of influences we have from rhythm and blues growing up in Los Angeles.'

Buster Brown's *Fannie Mae* made No.1 on the R&B charts in 1959.

sing **boy** **boys**

In the mid-'80s the Beach Boys were struggling with their image and attempting to make themselves relevant once again. They brought in Steve Levine to produce their album, giving it the inspiring title *The Beach Boys*. Steve's solution to the problem of how to get the Boys back on top was simple: drum machines and Fairlights. He also got two writers from his *succès de moment* to knock up a song for the band, which is how they came to sing *Passing Friend* written by Culture Club's Boy George and Roy Hay.

transatlantic
divide

An eleven-year-old boy stood on the corner of the street in deepest red neck Texas. He played his guitar, sang and collected money. In the end he made $20 but instead of taking it home to his family, who could well have done with it, he blew it on arcade machines. This was 1942 and by sixty years later he had recorded over 200 albums, which is probably a record in itself, and had 165 records on the *Billboard* country chart. George Jones is a legend in country music and he's never had a hit in the UK. The closest he came was when his ex-wife Tammy Wynette had a hit with *D.I.V.O.R.C.E* in 1975.

almost
famous

One of the more interesting(?) ideas of the '80s was the music press's decision to encourage unsigned bands to send in tapes of their efforts to be 'reviewed' by experts. *Melody Maker* called their page for aspiring artists 'Playback' and it regularly featured some literary gems along with some unintentionally funny stuff from the bands themselves. Take Hickory Wind, who were named after a Gram Parsons song: they listed their influences as Planxty, the Clash, Dylan and Dexy's Midnight Runners. They also featured two saxophones, which makes it difficult to see the Parsons connection. Among the songs they submitted for consideration was *What's Time To A Mole*. Unsurprisingly we've heard nothing from them since. Weird and wonderful group names abound; Adrian's Wall and Uncle Ian & The Tooth Decay give you a flavour of the times.

the
darkness

Paul Jones, the original singer with Manfred Mann, has some strange memories of the very first package tour they were on. 'We backed the Crystals on their first tour – forty-two gigs in forty-one days – many doubles. We had just released *54321* and so all the girls were screaming for us. The Crystals got quite upset, so when the Crystals were on, we had to stand still and play in the dark behind them.'

hello
darkness

In late 2002 composer Mike Batt (famous as the creator of the Wombles) paid over £100,000 to the publisher of the late John Cage's music. It was the price of silence. Batt used a minute's silence on his album *Classical Graffiti* and in a sense of fun credited it to Batt/Cage. John Cage was the American *enfant terrible* of the avant-garde who died in 1992, having forty years earlier composed a piece called *4'33"*, a work that consists of precisely that much silence. Live performances had a pianist sitting at the piano for the requisite time doing absolutely nothing: Cage reckoned it was his finest hour. During his lifetime Cage's acolytes played around with the idea, in the same way as he took ideas from others and included them in his work. Unfortunately Peters Edition, his publisher, have jealously guarded what they see as theirs and apparently the sound of silence is all down to J. Cage and Peters Edition. The payment Batt made to Peters Edition was almost certainly more than he made from sales of the album. It's a good job Paul and Art had the good sense to sing 'the Sound of Silence'.

keep awake **man!**

At the start of the new decade a group of German theologians, musicologists, philosophers, composers and organists got together in Halberstadt to discuss an exciting new project. It was the playing of the world's longest piece of music, and they plan it to last 639 years (the age of the Halberstadt organ in 2000). It was originally a 20-minute piece for piano written by John Cage and and entitled *As Slow As Possible*. Determined not to rush things they spent the first seventeen months pumping up the bellows of the organ. The first note was struck in February 2003. The third of the opening three notes is due to be played just as this book is published. Art for art's sake?

I'm desperate **for** change

The late '60s spawned some wonderful group names related to psychedelia – quite often a band's name was a whole lot better than the music they played. One outfit that might well fall into that category is the Changing Tyrannosaurus of Despair, whose drummer unfortunately demanded the name be altered. Not because it wouldn't fit on his kit, but because he 'couldn't relate to despair'. They became the Detroit Edison White Light Co. No relation, I'm sure, to Edison Lighthouse.

money-back **guarantee**

In 1994 27,000 people were offered a refund following Elvis Presley's failure to appear at a concert in Long Island on 22 August 1977. Elvis had died a few days earlier. There was one slight drawback as the applicants had to produce the ticket or some other proof of purchase in order to qualify. Suffice it to say you would get more on eBay from selling the ticket.

big might be beautiful . . . except for the traffic

The largest attendance at a rock festival was at 1983's US Festival near San Bernardino, California. It was organized by one of the co-founders of Apple, Steve Wozniak, and between 28 and 30 May 670,000 showed up to see David Bowie, U2, INXS and a whole host of others. The largest single-day crowd at a festival poured into Watkins Glen, New York, for the Summer Jam on 28 July 1973. More than 600,000 squeezed into the car race circuit to see bands including the Grateful Dead, the Allman Brothers and the Band. It's been claimed that this was the biggest gathering of people in America – ever. It means that on that day one in every 350 people in the US was there . . . and they can't all have been Dead Heads, can they?

left is right

Everyone knows that Paul McCartney and Jimi Hendrix are both left handed because they play their guitars that way. But so are Don and Phil Everly, Glen Campbell and Dick Dale. Then there's Black Sabbath's Tony Iommi, who's left handed but had to have special pads and a thimble-type cap fitted after he badly injured his right hand. Paul Simon, on the other hand, plays right handed but is actually left handed. Drummers Ringo Starr and Phil Collins are both left handed. But when Phil sings, rather like another left-handed singer, Robert Plant, it doesn't make any discernible difference.

— ONE-LINER —
Perry Como was the seventh son of a seventh son, Pietro Como.

mud sticks

Mud's name was chosen by guitarist Rob Davis. 'At the time we were all wearing kind of mud-coloured suede jackets which gave me the idea. It proved to be a good name because we always got big billing on posters advertising concerts even when we were way down the list. Among groups with longer names ours really stood out because, with only three letters, they had to print it bigger.'

public pronouncements

In our never-ending quest for the worst reviews of hit records we stumbled on a real corker. According to Allan Jones, the then assistant editor of the *Melody Maker*, this record was 'dull, not daring and quickly unlisten-able'. He had already pinned his colours to the mast by saying, 'This ridiculous epic is so comprehen-sively awful and clumsily pretentious that it's positively awe inspiring.' The year was 1982, the record Dire Straits' single *Private Invest-igations*. While Allan didn't say whether he thought it would be a hit or not, he clearly felt it didn't deserve to be. In fact it made No.2 on the charts, the highest position any Dire Straits single would ever achieve. The *Love Over Gold* album from which it was taken made No.1 in the UK and spent 200 weeks on the album charts. Mind you, Allan may just have been having a bad day because in the same issue he declared that Culture Club's *Do You Really Want to Hurt Me?* was 'woefully ordinary'. He claimed Boy George 'sang with all the camped up theatrical galumph of Kathy Kirby'. The song became the band's first No.1 in the UK and narrowly missed the top in America, staying at No.2 for three weeks.

kiss & tell

Back in 1979 Bill Aucoin, the then manager of Kiss, was heard to remark 'I don't think their egos are going to get in the way of their careers,' which was probably right because they went on to sell over 80 million records. At the same time Gene Simmons was worried that some of the other members of the band were getting chubby. He, of course, was probably not imagining they would still be doing it a quarter of a century later, by which time his own middle-aged girth would not be quite so appealing in the costumes or the make-up.

iSay

Ten years ago there was dancing in the street, nay jubilation of unprecedented proportions. All the big hi-fi makers were bringing out CD jukeboxes ('a wonderful piece of techno-convenience') that could hold around 100 CDs which played for over 100 hours. 'Almost 5 days without repeating a single tune', went the sales blurb. In their wildest dreams they could not have imagined the ipod!

queen in the regal sense

In 1973 one journalist wrote that with all the glam and glitter, Queen must be a gay band. So the question was raised: were they or weren't they? Another journalist then wrote, 'It transpired that they weren't, and were keen to play down the gay connotation of the name.' 'It's all very embarrassing,' admitted Queen's singer Freddie Mercury. 'Actually we've been around quite a while and we chose our name long before glam rock and the gay thing became fashionable. We like to think of ourself as Queen in the regal sense.'

big pub
bands

Everyone has to start somewhere and for many bands in the '60s and ever since 'somewhere' has been the pub. Well before the era of Pub Rock, bands frequented places like the Horse and Jockey in Mansfield, on stages that barely qualified as such. The Greyhound on the Brighton Road was another pub that for a while hosted many aspiring bands. Given that it was home to the Redhill and Reigate Arts Workshop it was hardly surprising. One Friday night the excitement was palpable. Walrus – a band about, it was said, to be signed to Decca Nova – were booked to appear. The tension, though, was more to do with how a nine-piece band that included brass and keyboards was going to fit on a stage that was normally pretty cosy for a four piece. That's what makes bands today hanker after playing 'clubs', it's the sense of being close to your audience (although some of Walrus were actually *in* the audience at the Greyhound).

Bands like the Stones are well known for their 'secret' club warm up gigs and during their last world tour they played in some intimate venues to recall their glory days, which is what makes the story of 1990s pub rockers Midlife Crisis so interesting. This group of ageing, mostly airline, executives, who had a fairly regular gig at the Ravenswood Arms Hotel, near East Grinstead, Sussex, decided that they were going to do the whole thing in reverse. They were not short of a bob or two so they pooled their cash, paid the required guarantee and booked the Royal Albert Hall for a gig in 1995. To a nearly full hall Midlife Crisis proved they were a really good pub rock band.

family
fortunes

Given the longevity of some bands, naming every member from down the years can be tricky. But there are some groups for whom it's practically impossible. Fleetwood Mac, of course, give you a head start with two names, but after the obvious Green, Christine McVie, Nicks and Buckingham it starts to get more difficult; especially when people like Dave Mason, formerly of Traffic, joined for just one album. In fact there are at least another dozen. Santana is another band that's a tough call, and that's not including all those people who turned up as guests on Carlos's recent albums. Perhaps worst of all is Fairport Convention, a band that truly defines dynastic. There have been upwards of thirty different Fairportees, with many leaving, coming back and leaving on multiple occasions during the almost forty years of their existence. For good measure chuck in the Byrds, the Mothers of Invention, and the Grateful Dead and you could keep yourself amused for hours.

rocket
mum

In the mid-'70s, Elton John was the first to modestly admit that much of his success was due to his writing partnership with Bernie Taupin. When they first met, Elton couldn't write lyrics and Bernie couldn't write music and anyway it was pure chance that brought them together at all. They met through a newspaper advertisement, but Bernie, having second thoughts after filling out the form, screwed it up and threw it into the wastepaper basket. But unbeknown to him his mother fished it out, uncrumpled it and stuck it in the post, thus bringing about some of the best songs of the '70s.

tango'd

Talking about the sea-change for the group marked by *Guitar Tango*, Shadows lead guitarist Hank Marvin confessed: 'Billy Connolly said that we were "ahead of our time", he said we were "ugly" before the Rolling Stones, "effeminate" before Boy George . . . and I think when we listen to *Guitar Tango* we prove him right because we went into the realms of being "unplugged", which MTV has just discovered, way back in 1962! At the time the *New Musical Express* etc. figured that we'd got it wrong by using acoustic guitars and sounding like an itinerant group of Spanish tango-ists.'

bend
it
bandits

When the record company releasing Dave Dee, Dozy, Beaky, Mick and Tich's singles in the States heard *Bend It*, they expressed serious concern over what they felt was an indecent lyric, so Dave and the guys tried to convince them that *Bend It* was a dance, scribbling down made-up steps on a piece of A4 paper. In a feeble attempt to prove their point they also changed a line to the really dreadful 'Bend it, bend it . . . all the kids in school can do it'. Knowing alterations might appease the Americans, record boss Jack Baverstock assembled the team from the US in his office to convince them of the record's innocent meaning. Unbeknown to Baverstock, the group had recorded special new lyrics written by Dave Dee for the occasion. 'We wrote the filthiest load of lyrics, four letter words and everything. Pure unadulterated filth! Jack Baverstock froze, but then wised up, dropped it in the bin and said, "Now can I have the real version?"'

so you wanna be a rock 'n' roll star?

Leader of the Byrds, Jim McGuinn, inexplicably changed his name to Roger in 1967. Not exactly the hippest name for a rock 'n' roll star during the summer of love, so there had to be a reason, right? Right. Indonesian guru Muhammad Subuh Sumohadi Widjojo, who founded the Subud faith, suggested to McGuinn that he change his first name to one beginning with R as it would reverberate better in the cosmos. The Byrds' front man toyed with the idea of becoming Rocket McGuinn and then Ramjet McGuinn, but eventually settled on Roger. He retains it to this day – a US DJ has Jim McGuinn registered with the American Federation of TV and Radio, so he can't revert to the name his parents gave him. In an interview with DJ Jim, Roger admitted that changing his name to one beginning with R hadn't really affected things at all.

just a bit of fun

In 1988 it was announced that Michael Jackson, who owns a high proportion of the publishing rights for Beatles back catalogue, was planning to make an animated film entitled *Strawberry Fields Forever*. The King of Pop (self-anointed) was planning to sing *Come Together*, among other songs. This was around the time that the tabloids were touting the story of MJ having to cancel a couple of gigs because his face was melting under the strength of the lights. Maybe that's why he was opting for a cartoon.

kiss this guy

Misheard lyrics are a fascinating source of chatter on the web, so much so that there are entire sites given over to them, like www.kissthisguy.com. It's inspired by Jimi Hendrix's lyrics to Purple Haze in which he sings ''scuse me while I kiss the sky'.

preparing
the pitch

Without question, Australian cricketer Don Bradman was one of the greatest batsmen of all time, so when Columbia Records asked him to commit something to record in 1930, they assumed they'd be getting some sort of talk on cricket. Not so, The Don surprised them with two songs, which were subsequently released – *An Old-Fashioned Locket* and *Our Bungalow of Dreams*.

it's
just
not
cricket

Football has had a long association with the singles charts. Whether it be the England squad, Waddle & Hoddle's appalling *Diamond Lights*, Kevin Keegan's equally dodgy rendition of *Head Over Heels In Love* or Des Lynam & the Wimbledon Choral Society's *World Cup '98 – Pavane*. Cricket on the other hand has been poorly served with only two known chart forays – the England Supporters Band's version of *The Great Escape* and England's Barmy Army, all 5,000 of them, singing *Come on England*, which staggered to No.45 for just a week in 1999.

jim'll
fix hit

Disc Jockey Jimmy Savile only ever made one record, a cover of Ray Stevens's US No.1 *Ahab The Arab*, which failed to chart, but sold over 13,000 copies. It became one of the earliest charity records – the eccentric Yorkshireman gave all the money to the Little Sisters of the Poor in Leeds. Ten years on Savile commented, 'The voice? It's good. I've got a pretty good voice, as it 'appens. I could still make a reasonable record, but I don't particularly want to. There are many people even in this day and age who wish they could sell 13,000 records.'

— QUESTIONS DEMANDING AN ANSWER # 6 —
Is there a worse track on a classic album than *Yellow Submarine* on the Beatles Revolver?

corporate
crime

According to Andy Gill, Gail Ann Dorsey's debut album *The Corporate World*, released in 1988 was going 'to get her touted, quite justifiably, as the female equivalent of Terence Trent D'Arby or Prince. Marshalling her many talents – strong lead vocals, perfect backing vocals, varied guitar styles, the occasional bass parts and a natural song writing gift. . . . If you thought you've already heard the debut album of the year, think again.' The album failed to chart either in Britain or America, and Gail didn't have a single in the charts on either side of the Atlantic. Having said all that, Gail Ann is in big demand as a session player and has been a member of David Bowie's band since 1995.

where
is she
now?

Tanita Tikaram's *Ancient Heart*, her 1988 debut album, got to No.3 on the UK album chart where it spent forty-nine weeks, notching up well over 2 million sales in the process. Over the course of the next ten years her four albums managed only thirteen weeks in total on the chart.

connected

Nina & Frederik – they of *Little Donkey* and *Sucu Sucu* fame – were both well-connected Scandinavians. Frederik was born Baron Frederik van Pallendt, his father was the Dutch ambassador to Denmark and his mother was the former Countess Bluecher-Altona. Nina's mother, Mrs Moller-Hasselbolch, was a society hostess. In 1958 King Frederik and Queen Ingrid of Denmark asked them to perform for the eighteenth birthday of Princess Margretha.

we're gonna make you a star

In the 1950s the American music industry was hit by a series of payola scandals in which cash was paid to DJs for playing particular records. This practice was subsequently outlawed, encouraging companies to find more subtle ways to plug their records. In 2004 they hit upon one – but it wasn't very subtle. One week in May, Canadian singer Avril Lavigne's record *Don't Tell Me* was played over 100 times on a Nashville radio station. In the early hours of one particular day the 3½-minute song aired eighteen times, sometimes just 11 minutes apart. This was all perfectly legal because Arista records was paying the radio station for advertising time. The reason it is so important is that in the US the charts are predicated on a mix of sales and airplay. *Billboard* also has a radio chart, which programme controllers across the country monitor to see which breaking records are hot. All in all it's a very worrying development, and Avril's record was not the first. The same had been done for other artists, including Sheryl Crowe.

final tap

In the summer of '65 the Rolling Stones went to No.1 in the US with *Satisfaction* and stayed there for a month. It might have been longer but for the fact that Hermitmania (strictly speaking an oxymoron) was in full swing, and Herman and the Hermits' *I'm Henry The VIII I Am* knocked the Stones from the top. By the following year things were waning for Herman but they were still playing some big shows throughout the US. One night they were topping the bill in Hawaii and the Who, on their first tour of the USA, were one of the support bands They were also keen practical jokers. When Herman and the Hermits got to the end of their last number, *Henry the VIII*, drummer Barry Whitwam's kit exploded. The Who, probably led by Keith Moon, and their roadies had used some left over pyros and gunpowder and wired it up. They set it off just as Whitwam hit the skins at the end of the song.

cash
goes camp

Every year old stars are rediscovered and put into that special category reserved for people who have paid their dues. Their careers are reassessed and they are allocated a place at the top table as the elder statesmen of not just their genre but of popular music as a whole. Johnny Cash gained admittance sometime around 1994 following the release of his highly acclaimed album *American Recordings*. But just as in life there was darkness before the dawn. In February 1993 Johnny Cash played a weekend booking at Butlins Holiday camp in Bognor Regis (half board £61 for the weekend, £26 self-catering). These Butlins weekends have become a regular off-season filler for a range of artists and as often as not feature '60s shows or soul weekends. Few have featured legends like the Man in Black.

slick **by** name,
slick by nature

The whole subject of celebrity children's names is a tricky area to explore and one entered into with a fair degree of trepidation. It's much like catwalk fashion – the rich and famous choose names that the rest of us amend and adapt for our own use. Musicians have always led the field when it comes to crazy names, although Moon Unit Zappa seems to have inspired no one . . . yet. One of the enduring urban legends concerns Jefferson Airplane/Starship partners and lovers, Grace Slick and Paul Kantner. They had a daughter in 1971 and when a nurse asked Grace what the baby was called her response caused some confusion. 'I noticed a crucifix around her neck and spontaneously said, "god. We spell it with a small g because we want her to be humble."' In actual fact when it came down to it they named her China. A few years earlier Michelle Phillips of the Mamas & Papas had named her daughter Chynna (now in Wilson Phillips with Brian Wilson's daughters, Carnie and Wendy).

the
british
invasion

At the spearhead of the legendary invasion of America by British artists were, as everyone knows, the Beatles. *I Want To Hold You Hand* made No.1 in early 1964 having first entered the charts on 18 January. They were not the first British group to find success in America: just a couple of weeks earlier the Caravelles (named after the French passenger airliner) made it to No.3 with *You Don't Have To Be A Baby To Cry*. With blurred hindsight people tend to put the Rolling Stones in the vanguard of the invasion but it would be ten months before they scored their first American top 10 hit with *Time is on My Side*. In addition to the Beatles, it was the Dave Clark Five who helped establish the bridgehead for British bands in America. Before the Stones' top 10 hit the beaming boys from Tottenham had six American top 20 hits including *Bits And Pieces*, *Can't You See That She's Mine* and *Because*, which all made the top 5. Before 1964 was over the Beatles had fifteen records on the US charts, seven of which made the top – a feat that has never been bettered in a single year.

some
call
it **wit**

Many album titles have vied for the accolade of 'worst of all time' but a strong contender is Landscape's 1981 offering *From the Tea Rooms Of Mars to The Hellholes Of Uranus*. It followed on nicely from a string of very different singles from this British band. Their first was *U2XME1X2MUC* in 1978, which failed to chart, and their first hit was *Einstein A Go Go*, which reached No.5. The latter included snatches of calls in which various members of the band tried, unsuccessfully, to reach President Ronald Reagan on the telephone.

repeat to fade repeat to fade repeat to fade repeat to fade repeat
to fade repeat to fade repeat to fade repeat to fade repeat to fade
repeat to fade repeat to fade repeat to fade repeat to fade repeat
to fade repeat to fade repeat to fade repeat to fade repeat to fade
repeat to fade repeat to fade repeat to fade repeat to fade repeat
to fade repeat to fade repeat to fade repeat to fade repeat to fade
repeat to fade repeat to fade repeat to fade repeat to fade repeat
to fade repeat to fade repeat to fade repeat to fade repeat to fade
repeat to fade repeat to fade repeat to fade repeat to fade repeat
to fade repeat to fade repeat to fade repeat to fade repeat to fade
repeat to fade repeat to fade repeat to fade repeat to fade repeat
to fade repeat to fade repeat to fade repeat to fade repeat to fade
repeat to fade repeat to fade repeat to fade repeat to fade repeat
to fade repeat to fade repeat to fade repeat to fade repeat to fade
repeat to fade repeat to fade repeat to fade repeat to fade repeat
to fade repeat to fade repeat to fade repeat to fade repeat to fade
repeat to fade repeat to fade repeat to fade repeat to fade repeat
to fade repeat to fade repeat to fade repeat to fade repeat to fade
repeat to fade repeat to fade repeat to fade repeat to fade repeat
to fade repeat to fade repeat to fade repeat to fade repeat to fade
repeat to fade repeat to fade repeat to fade repeat to fade repeat
to fade repeat to fade repeat to fade repeat to fade repeat to fade
repeat to fade repeat to fade repeat to fade repeat to fade repeat
to fade repeat to fade repeat to fade repeat to fade repeat to fade
repeat to fade repeat to fade repeat to fade repeat to fade repeat
to fade repeat to fade repeat to fade repeat to fade repeat to fade
repeat to fade repeat to fade repeat to fade repeat to fade repeat
to fade repeat to fade repeat to fade repeat to fade repeat to fade
repeat to fade repeat to fade repeat to fade repeat to fade repeat
to fade repeat to fade repeat to fade epeat to fade repeat to fade
repeat to fade repeat to fade repeat to fade repeat to fade repeat
to fade repeat to fade repeat to fade repeat to fade repeat to fade
repeat to fade repeat to fade repeat to fade repeat to fade repeat
to fade repeat to fade repeat to fade repeat to fade repeat to fade
repeat to fade repeat to fade repeat to fade repeat to fade repeat